EMPOWERED EDUCATORS IN SINGAPORE

How High-Performing Systems Shape Teaching Quality

A. Lin Goodwin, Ee-Ling Low, Linda Darling-Hammond

JOSSEY-BASS™
A Wiley Brand

Published by Jossey-Bass
A Wiley Brand

One Montgomery Street, Suite 1000, San Francisco, CA 94104-4594—www.josseybass.com

Jossey-Bass books and products are available through most bookstores. To contact Jossey-Bass directly call our Customer Care Department within the U.S. at 800-956-7739, outside the U.S. at 317-572-3986, or fax 317-572-4002.

Wiley publishes in a variety of print and electronic formats and by print-on-demand. Some material included with standard print versions of this book may not be included in e-books or in print-on-demand. If this book refers to media such as a CD or DVD that is not included in the version you purchased, you may download this material at http://booksupport.wiley.com. For more information about Wiley products, visit www .wiley.com.

ISBN: 9781119369721
ISBN: 9781119369738
ISBN: 9781119369745

Cover design by Wiley
Cover image: © suriya9/Getty Images, Inc.

FIRST EDITION
PB Printingg 10 9 8 7 6 5 4 3 2 1

CONTENTS

FOREWORD

FEW WOULD DISAGREE THAT, among all the factors that affect how much students learn, the quality of their teachers ranks very high. But what, exactly, do policy makers, universities, and school leaders need to do to make sure that the vast majority of teachers in their jurisdiction are *literally* world class?

Perhaps the best way to answer that question is to look carefully and in great detail at what the countries whose students are performing at the world's top levels are doing to attract the highest quality high school students to teaching careers, prepare them well for that career, organize schools so teachers can do the best work of which they are capable, and provide incentives for them to get better at the work before they finally retire.

It was not hard for us to find the right person to lead a study that would do just that. Stanford professor Linda Darling-Hammond is one of the world's most admired researchers. Teachers and teaching have been lifelong professional preoccupations for her. And, not least, Professor Darling-Hammond is no stranger to international comparative studies. Fortunately for us and for you, she agreed to lead an international comparative study of teacher quality in a selection of top-performing countries. The study, *Empowered Educators: How High-Performing Systems Shape Teaching Quality Around the World*, took two years to complete and is unprecedented in scope and scale.

The volume you are reading is one of six books, including case studies conducted in Australia, Canada, China, Finland, and Singapore. In addition to the case studies and the cross-study analysis, the researchers have collected a range of videos and artifacts (http://ncee.org/empowered-educators)—ranging from a detailed look at how the daily schedules of teachers in Singapore ensure ample time for collaboration and planning to a description of the way Shanghai teachers publish their classroom research in refereed journals—that we hope will be of great value to policy makers and educators interested in using and adapting the tools that the top-performing jurisdictions use to get the highest levels of teacher quality in the world.

Studies of this sort are often done by leading scholars who assemble hordes of graduate students to do the actual work, producing reams of reports framed by the research plan, which are then analyzed by the principal investigator. That is not what happened in this case. For this report, Professor Darling-Hammond recruited two lead researcher-writers for each case study, both senior, one from the country being studied and one from another country, including top-level designers and implementers of the systems being studied and leading researchers. This combination of insiders and external observers, scholars and practitioner-policy makers, gives this study a depth, range, and authenticity that is highly unusual.

But this was not just an effort to produce first-class case studies. The aim was to understand what the leaders were doing to restructure the profession of teaching for top performance. The idea was to cast light on that by examining what was the same and what was different from country to country to see if there were common threads that could explain uncommon results. As the data-gathering proceeded, Professor Darling-Hammond brought her team together to exchange data, compare insights, and argue about what the data meant. Those conversations, taking place among a remarkable group of senior policy actors, practitioners, and university-based researchers from all over the world, give this work a richness rarely achieved in this sort of study.

The researchers examined all sorts of existing research literature on the systems they were studying, interviewed dozens of people at every level of the target systems, looked at everything from policy at the national level to practice in individual schools, and investigated not only the specific policies and practices directly related to teacher quality, but the larger economic, political, institutional, and cultural contexts in which policies on teacher quality are shaped.

Through it all, what emerges is a picture of a sea change taking place in the paradigm of mass education in the advanced industrial nations. When university graduates of any kind were scarce and most people had jobs requiring only modest academic skills, countries needed teachers who knew little more than the average high school graduate, perhaps less than that at the primary school level. It was not too hard to find capable people, typically women, to do that work, because the job opportunities for women with that level of education were limited.

But none of that is true anymore. Wage levels in the advanced industrial countries are typically higher than elsewhere in the world. Employers who can locate their manufacturing plants and offices anywhere in the world and who do not need highly skilled labor look for workers who have the basic skills they need in low-wage countries, so the work available to workers with only the basic skills in the high-wage countries is drying up. That process is being greatly accelerated by the rapid advance of automation. The jobs that are left in the high-wage countries mostly demand a higher level of more complex skills.

These developments have put enormous pressure on the governments of high-wage countries to find teachers who have more knowledge and a deeper command of complex skills. These are the people who can get into selective universities and go into occupations that have traditionally had higher status and are better compensated than school teaching. What distinguishes the countries with the best-performing education systems is that: 1) they have figured this out and focused hard on how to respond to these new realities; and 2) they have succeeded not just in coming up with promising designs for the systems they need but in implementing those systems well. The result is not only profound changes in the way they source, educate, train, and support a truly professional teaching force, but schools in which the work of teachers is very differently organized, the demands on school leaders is radically changed, teachers become not the recipient of a new set of instructions from the "center," but the people who are actually responsible for designing and carrying out the reforms that are lifting the performance of their students every day. Not least important, these systems offer real careers in teaching that enable teachers, like professionals in other fields, to gain more authority, responsibility, compensation, and status as they get better and better at the work, without leaving teaching.

This is an exciting story. It is the story that you are holding in your hand. The story is different in every country, province, and state. But the themes behind the stories are stunningly similar. If you find this work only half as compelling as I have, you will be glued to these pages.

Marc Tucker, President
National Center on Education and the Economy

ACKNOWLEDGMENTS

IN SINGAPORE, a frequent and common refrain from the time of independence has been that people are the country's "most precious resource." Throughout this project, people have been our most precious resource and have given whole-heartedly of themselves to support our work in telling the story of teaching, learning, and schooling in "the little red dot." First of all, we could not have begun to weave an authentic and compelling story if not for the schools that opened their doors to us and offered us the opportunity to join their communities for a while. Thank you Kranji Secondary School, Raffles Girls' School, and Ngee Ann Secondary School—being immersed in your vibrant, caring, and energetic environments was a true education.

Of course wonderful people are at the heart of wonderful schools, so our deep thanks go to the fine school leaders who welcomed us in. At Raffles Girls' School, special thanks go to Principal Mrs. Poh Mun See, Senior Deputy Principal Mrs. Shirley Tan, and Director, Centre for Pedagogical Research and Learning Mrs. Mary George Cheriyan. We are equally grateful to Principal Ms. Tan Hwee Pin, Vice Principal Mrs. Punitha Ramanan, and Head of Department Ms. Serene Lai Woon Mui at Kranji Secondary School. We appreciate your support in smoothing the way for our interviews and filming, as well as your willingness to allow us to observe different conversations and meetings. Your professional discussions taught us a great deal about how you foster collegial decision making and collaboration in your respective schools. And finally, an extra shout out to all of you at Kranji for graciously RE-opening your doors to us when additional footage was needed. We are deeply appreciative of your generosity of spirit and collegiality.

We also want to express our thanks to all the teachers and the pupils in each school—we know we were hard to ignore, especially our cameras and microphones, but you managed to carry on doing what you do so well—teaching, learning, and collaborating—allowing us to capture a flavor of the rich and meaningful curriculum you offer or experience. Extra special thanks go to two educators in particular, Senior Teacher Mdm. Rosmiliah Bte Kasmin of Kranji Secondary School, and Teacher-Specialist Mr. Azahar Bin Mohamed Noor of Raffles Girls' School. We are deeply indebted to you for patiently enduring our many questions, our presence, our equipment and our cameras in your classrooms, and our disruption of your schedule. We know what a priceless gift you each gave us in generously inviting us to witness your practice and hear you talk aloud about your passions, goals, and your pedagogical decision-making. Our special thanks also go to Master Teachers Ms. Cynthia Seto and Ms. Irene Tan at the Academy of Singapore Teachers for your insightful sharing on the teacher-led culture of professional learning in Singapore. All of you are such exemplary teachers that to say we learned *so* much about quality teaching is a huge understatement—a special thank you in all four co-official languages of Singapore is a must: Terima Kasih, 谢谢, Nandri, Thank You!

This acknowledgment would not be complete without a note of gratitude to colleagues in the Ministry of Education in Singapore. We appreciated your support every step along the way and your keen eyes on rough cuts of the videos. Thank you for your feedback and wise counsel. We are indebted to the Ford Foundation for generously funding the videotaping work—thank you for supporting this essential aspect of our study. Thanks also are due to Mr. Steve Tan. We could not have asked for a more accommodating videographer who was able to discern the best footage we needed, even when we were not entirely certain ourselves. We also would like to express our appreciation to Barnett Berry and the Center for Teaching Quality for their support and collaboration.

Finally, but far from least, bucket loads of accolades and thanks go to the Singapore research associates who were our thought partners, colleagues, support systems: (alphabetically) Hui Chenri and Jane Lin Huiling, we could not have done this without you both—you helped us in so many countless ways by sorting through ideas with us, keeping us on track with deadlines and focused on the tasks at hand, searching through literature, gathering documents, organizing school visits, collecting data, and even comfort cooking and feeding when the going got tough! We cannot say thank you enough. Our U.S. graduate assistants also deserve our deep appreciation for their help in gathering and reviewing literature, and finding the best images for colorful and attractive PowerPoint presentations—thank you so much Kelsey Darity and Crystal Chen.

This has been an engrossing and fascinating project that clearly could not have been accomplished without the kind support of many wonderful people. Here's a final bow to everyone. The best of the Singapore story comes from all of them, while the fault of any errors or omissions remains entirely ours.

Note: Designations that appear throughout the book reflect personnel at the point when the research was conducted.

ABOUT THE SPONSORING ORGANIZATIONS

THIS WORK IS MADE POSSIBLE through a grant by the Center on International Education Benchmarking® of the National Center on Education and the Economy® and is part of a series of reports on teacher quality systems around the world. For a complete listing of the material produced by this research program, please visit www.ncee.org/cieb.

The Center on International Education Benchmarking®, a program of NCEE, funds and conducts research around the world on the most successful education systems to identify the strategies those countries have used to produce their superior performance. Through its books, reports, website, monthly newsletter, and a weekly update of education news around the world, CIEB provides up-to-date information and analysis on those countries whose students regularly top the PISA league tables. Visit www.ncee.org/cieb to learn more.

The National Center on Education and the Economy was created in 1988 to analyze the implications of changes in the international economy for American education, formulate an agenda for American education based on that analysis and seek wherever possible to accomplish that agenda through policy change and development of the resources educators would need to carry it out. For more information visit www.ncee.org.

Research for this volume was coordinated by the Stanford Center for Opportunity Policy in Education (SCOPE) at Stanford University. SCOPE was founded in 2008 to foster research, policy, and practice to advance high-quality, equitable education systems in the United States and internationally.

ABOUT THE AUTHORS

A. Lin Goodwin is the Evenden Professor of Education, and vice dean at Teachers College, Columbia University, New York. She is immediate past vice president of the American Educational Research Association (AERA)—Division K: Teaching and Teacher Education (2013–2016). In 2015, she was honored as a Distinguished Researcher by AERA's Special Interest Group: Research on the Education of Asian and Pacific Americans, and was named the inaugural Dr. Ruth Wong Professor of Teacher Education by the National Institute of Education, Singapore.

Dr. Goodwin's research focuses on teacher and teacher educator identities and development; multicultural understandings and curriculum enactments; issues facing Asian/Asian American teachers and students in U.S. schools; and on international analyses/comparisons of teacher education practice and policy. Her work appears in top journals including the *Journal of Teacher Education, Urban Education,* and *Teachers College Record*. An international consultant around issues of teacher education, Dr. Goodwin is currently working with educators in Poland, Thailand, and Singapore.

Professor **Ee-Ling Low** is head of Strategic Planning and Academic Quality at the National Institute of Education, Singapore. She was the associate dean of Teacher Education from 2009–2013. She obtained her PhD in Linguistics (Acoustic Phonetics) from the University of Cambridge, UK, under the university's Overseas Graduate Scholarship award. She won the Fulbright Advanced Research Scholarship in 2008 which she spent at the Lynch School of Education at Boston College. She played a leading role in the conceptualization of the NIE Strategic Roadmap: Towards 2017 and the development of the Teacher Education for the 21st Century (TE^{21}) model. In 2012, she was awarded the

Public Administration Medal (Bronze) by the president of the Republic of Singapore for her dedication and commitment toward furthering the cause of education in Singapore. She is Singapore's representative in Stanford University's International Teacher Policy Study and Harvard Graduate School of Education's Global Education Innovation Initiative.

Linda Darling-Hammond, president of the Learning Policy Institute, is the Charles E. Ducommun Professor of Education Emeritus at Stanford University, where she founded the Stanford Center for Opportunity Policy in Education and served as the faculty sponsor of the Stanford Teacher Education Program, which she helped to redesign.

Darling-Hammond is past president of the American Educational Research Association and recipient of its awards for Distinguished Contributions to Research, Lifetime Achievement, Research Review, and Research-to-Policy. She is also a member of the American Association of Arts and Sciences and of the National Academy of Education. From 1994–2001, she was executive director of the National Commission on Teaching and America's Future, whose 1996 report *What Matters Most: Teaching for America's Future* was named one of the most influential reports affecting U.S. education in that decade. In 2006, Darling-Hammond was named one of the nation's ten most influential people affecting educational policy. In 2008, she served as the leader of President Barack Obama's education policy transition team.

Dr. Darling-Hammond began her career as a public school teacher and co-founded both a preschool and a public high school. She has consulted widely with federal, state, and local officials and educators on strategies for improving education policies and practices. Among her more than 500 publications are a number of award-winning books, including *The Right to Learn, Teaching as the Learning Profession, Preparing Teachers for a Changing World*, and *The Flat World and Education*. She received an Ed.D. from Temple University (with highest distinction) and a B.A. from Yale University (magna cum laude).

ONLINE DOCUMENTS AND VIDEOS

Access online documents and videos at
http://ncee.org/empowered-educators 

Link Number	Description	URL
1	Video: Day in the Life of a Singaporean Teacher	http://ncee.org/2016/12/video-day-in-the-life-of-a-singaporean-teacher/
2	Singapore Desired Outcomes of Education	http://ncee.org/2017/01/singapore-desired-outcomes-of-education/
3	21st Century Competencies	
4	Singapore Thinking Schools, Learning Nation	http://ncee.org/2017/01/singapore-thinking-schools-learning-nation/
5	Singapore Teach Less, Learn More	http://ncee.org/2017/01/singapore-teach-less-learn-more/
6	Video: Azahar Bin Mohd Noor on Student Research	http://ncee.org/2017/01/video-azahar-bin-mohd-noor-on-student-research/
7	Singapore Holistic Education	http://ncee.org/2017/01/singapore-holistic-education/
8	Bachelor of Arts (Education)/Bachelor of Science (Education)	https://www.moe.gov.sg/careers/teach/teacher-training-schemes/bachelor-of-arts-(education)-bachelor-of-science-(education)
9	Diploma in Education	https://www.moe.gov.sg/careers/teach/teacher-training-schemes/diploma-in-education
10	Teacher Training Schemes for Tamil, Art, Music and Chinese	https://www.moe.gov.sg/careers/teach/teacher-training-schemes/teacher-training-schemes-for-tamil-art-music-and-chinese
11	Singapore Handbook for Teacher Education Programs	http://ncee.org/2017/01/singapore-handbook-for-teacher-education-programs/

Link Number	Description	URL
12	Skillful Teaching and Enhanced Mentoring (STEM) Program	
13	Video: Miss Tan Hwee Pin on Teacher Evaluation	http://ncee.org/2017/01/video-miss-tan-hwee-pin-on-teacher-evaluation/
14	Video: Rosmiliah Bte Kasmin	http://ncee.org/2016/12/video-rosmiliah-bte-kasmin/
15	Video: Mary George Cheriyan on Advanced Study	http://ncee.org/2017/01/video-mary-george-cheriyan-on-advanced-study/
16	Video: Azahar Bin Mohd Noor, Part 1	http://ncee.org/2016/12/video-azahar-bin-mohd-noor-part-1/
17	Video: Tan Hwee Pin, Part 1	http://ncee.org/2016/12/video-tan-hwee-pin-part-1/
18	Video: Mary George Cheriyan on Professional Learning	http://ncee.org/2017/01/video-mary-george-cheriyan-on-professional-learning/
19	Video: Azahar Bin Mohd Noor on Student Feedback	http://ncee.org/2017/01/video-azahar-bin-mohd-noor-on-student-feedback/
20	Education Service Professional Development and Career Plan	

SINGAPORE: FROM "WHO?" TO "WHO'S WHO!"

IT WAS NOT SO LONG AGO that Singapore was a little known place in "the Far East," with most Westerners operating under the misconception that it was part of China or Hong Kong, completely unaware of its status as an independent country/city state. This changed when Singapore's education system became globally prominent as Singaporean students topped the international rankings in mathematics and science achievement in the 2003 Trends in International Mathematics and Science Study (TIMSS). More significantly, 90% of the student population who took this test achieved scores that were above the international median score. This achievement was especially noteworthy because, even though English has been used as a medium of instruction in all Singapore schools since 1987 (most Singapore schools were using English as the medium of instruction by the 1970s), it is not the home language for many Singaporean students. As of the most recent census in 2010, only 45.4% of individual children between the ages of 5 and 19 years live in homes where English is most frequently spoken (Department of Statistics, 2010).

Singaporean students have routinely outperformed their peers in scores of countries around the world, including the United States, regularly performing at or near the top in a range of international assessments. In the Progress in International Reading Literacy Study (PIRLS) conducted in 2011, Singapore students ranked fourth among 49 nations in terms of literacy performance (Mullis, Martin, Foy, & Drucker, 2012). In the 2015 Program for International Student Assessment (PISA) results, of the 65 participating education systems in the paper-based assessment component, Singapore ranked at the top in Mathematics, Reading, and Science Literacy skills (OECD, 2016). In 2015, Singapore topped 76 countries in the Organisation for Economic Co-operation and Development (OECD) global school rankings, followed by Hong Kong and South Korea, which ranked second and third place, respectively (Coughlan, 2015). The latest TIMSS data from 2015 indicate that this trend continues: fourth and eighth graders in Singapore placed first on the mathematics and science assessments (Provasnik, Malley, Stephens, Landeros, Perkins, & Tang, 2016).

As a consequence of the high rankings of its students in these international comparisons, Singapore now enjoys much wider recognition worldwide and rising status as a global player, both educationally and economically. The consistently strong performance of its pupils, coupled with its high level of purchasing power parities (PPP)—which ranked seventh globally, just behind the United States (World Bank, 2008)—and its transformation, literally, from a developing country into a developed country in a single generation, has changed the question from "Where is Singapore?" to "What is Singapore doing?"

Singapore's status as a highly performing education system has led to many international peers clamoring to know the "Singapore secret," as if her strong showing on international assessments could be attributed to some concrete, exportable, isolated, expeditious, or simple policy or strategy. The reality is that Singapore has only recently become synonymous with educational excellence, and this excellence is the consequence of a strategic and concerted nationwide effort to improve education, spanning about 25 years. So rather than a miracle tale, this is the story of how a tiny city-state, affectionately called "the red dot" by its citizens—because that is how the country appears on world maps—has reached impressive heights of both educational and economic success in the absence of natural resources of any kind. More specifically, this case study of Singapore illuminates what it means or how it looks to engage in systemic, long-term and ongoing, consistent, and deliberative reform of schools and schooling, in the midst of nation building and postcolonial independence, with a particular focus on quality teachers as the key to educational excellence.

We begin this case study by briefly providing some basic background information about Singapore in terms of history, relevant demographics, the sociopolitical context, governance, and education. Against this general backdrop, we broadly map out the Singapore school system and the different pathways and opportunities available to students as they progress through the various grades and levels of schooling. We couple this mapping with an overview of the current educational context in Singapore, including some key priorities/goals. We then narrow our focus to look specifically at teachers and teaching policy in order to understand at a level of greater detail—how teachers are recruited, prepared, nurtured, and in that process, sustained and retained.

We organize this discussion under five key themes that emerged from this case study as central to the development and support of a quality teaching force that supports and enacts a quality education system: (1) a clear vision and belief in the centrality of education; (2) a systemic approach to innovation, reform, and change; (3) coherent investments in a high-quality teaching force; (4) educative and developmental appraisal; (5) a learning system and a learning profession. The first two themes provide a frame for the larger educational context, a way to conceptualize the innovations and reforms that have taken place most recently. The other three themes help us talk about teachers and teaching quality specifically. It is important to note though, that given Singapore's systemic approach to innovation, reform, and change, the themes cannot be thought of as isolated from one another; in fact, they are interwoven in our narrative because all of them are occurring in tandem. Singapore's management of education needs to be perceived as an evolving, intersecting whole, rather than a set of separate, disconnected initiatives.

To help us tell the story, we use data from government documents and interviews with policy makers and higher education officials, as well as school observations and interviews with teachers and principals—especially Kranji Secondary School (government) (Link 1) and Raffles Girls' School (independent)—to provide authentic portraits and perspectives that illustrate how these themes are enacted in real settings. We conclude the case by reflecting on what we have learned and by offering a preview of what is percolating in Singapore in terms of goals and new directions for teachers.

Singapore in Brief: Background and Essential Information

Singapore is a very small Southeast Asian country, a 716 square kilometer island (Department of Statistics, n.d.) bookended by the southern tip of the Malayan peninsula 1 kilometer to the north, and the nearest Indonesian island about 20 kilometers to the south. The People's Action Party (PAP) has been the country's governing political party since divestment from British colonial rule in 1959. It continued as the governing party when Singapore became an independent nation in August 1965, following brief membership in the Malaysian Federation between 1963 and 1965.

"Singapore is a sovereign republic, with a legal system based on the English common law" (Gill, 2013, p. 3), and thus follows a parliamentary system of government headed by the prime minister. The current prime minister is Lee Hsien Loong, who has held this elected position since 2004; Dr. Tony Tan Keng Yam is, at present, Singapore's elected president.

The physical landscape of Singapore is decidedly vertical, densely packed with hundreds of commercial skyscrapers and housing development blocks (i.e., government housing) where the majority of Singaporeans live, etched with an intricate network of roads and highways supporting a well-developed and efficient public transportation system—both above ground and below. As a modern, technologically advanced city-state, it displays many of the characteristics and trappings of urbanicity—throngs of people, an overabundance of vehicles, hypercommercialism, limited space, and a great diversity in terms of people, languages, cultures, food, traditions, and ways of life.

Uncharacteristic of many urban centers, Singapore is also a clean, manicured, garden city, well organized and planned, efficient, with low levels of crime and poverty. Much of the population is middle class and enjoys high standards of living including excellent health facilities, well-equipped and safe schools, smooth-running and efficient provision of government services, public housing that is ever more sophisticated and amenity-rich, and myriad opportunities and options for professional, intellectual, and personal advancement.

Compulsory education regardless of race, language, or religion ensures that each child is given the full opportunity to succeed and the system rides mainly on the principles of meritocracy. The Singapore story is quite different from some other high-performing countries, which are largely homogenous; its multiracial, multiethnic, and multireligious population of about 5.61 million comprises a Chinese majority (74.3%), Malays (13.4%), and Indians (9.1%) (Department of Statistics, 2016). The four co-official languages are Malay, Tamil, Chinese (Mandarin), and English. All Singaporean students can be considered as English-knowing bilinguals—English is taught explicitly in schools along with one's ethnic mother tongue.

Before delving into the five main themes emerging from our case study, we will spend some time talking about the Singapore school system and the main educational initiatives in order to provide the contextual background to our study.

The Singapore School System: Many Pathways, One Goal

Singapore has in place many academic pathways in order to ensure that the potential of every child can be developed to the fullest. The pathways cater to those who not only demonstrate academic strength but other strengths as well. More fundamentally, there is a clear aim to equip every person with basic skills so that each is employable and able to earn a decent living, thus helping to reduce poverty and empowering every citizen to maximize his/her life's potential.

To achieve this aspiration, Singapore has established a comprehensive education system from preschool to university, as well as continuing education and on-the-job training. The system consists of five major phases: preschool (4–6 years old), primary (7–12 years old), secondary (13–16/17 years old), postsecondary (17–19 years old), university (20–23 years old), and continuing education and training (CET; Ministry of Education (MOE), n.d.g.). This educational map is depicted in detail in Figure 1.

Virtually everyone completes some postsecondary education. Students are also encouraged and frequently supported via scholarships, offered by public and private sectors, to attend college overseas. About 74% of young people complete postsecondary education in a college or a polytechnic, and nearly all of the remainder go on to pursue vocational education at the Institute of Technical Education (ITE) with three colleges, which offers them a certificate or a diploma in fields that allow them to find employment in the many multinational companies/industries that are based in Singapore. Education statistics (MOE, 2014) show that about 28% of the primary 1 cohort pursue grades 11 and 12 at a junior college, the majority of whom go on to complete a university degree; about 46% of each cohort embark on a three-year polytechnic education culminating in a diploma. About half of the polytechnic graduates continue on to pursue a university degree (often moving directly into the second year at university if they pursue a related discipline at the university level), while the other half go out into the job market and are employed mainly in the technical and engineering fields. Among the remaining 21% of each cohort who pursue vocational education at the Institute of Technical Education for two years, some go on to pursue a polytechnic diploma with a fraction subsequently embarking on a university degree, while others go into the workplace.

The preschool (noncompulsory) phase lasts for up to three years, after which students go through six years of compulsory (and free) primary school education. Based on their interests, the manpower needs determined by the government and industry, and their grades obtained at 6th grade (otherwise defined as when they have completed primary school), several academic pathways are open to Singaporean students. The majority join secondary schools (13–16 years old or secondary 1, 2, 3, and 4), which consist of three main streams of study: (1) the four-year express stream; (2) the five-year normal academic stream; and (3) the four-year

Figure 1. The Singapore Education Landscape.

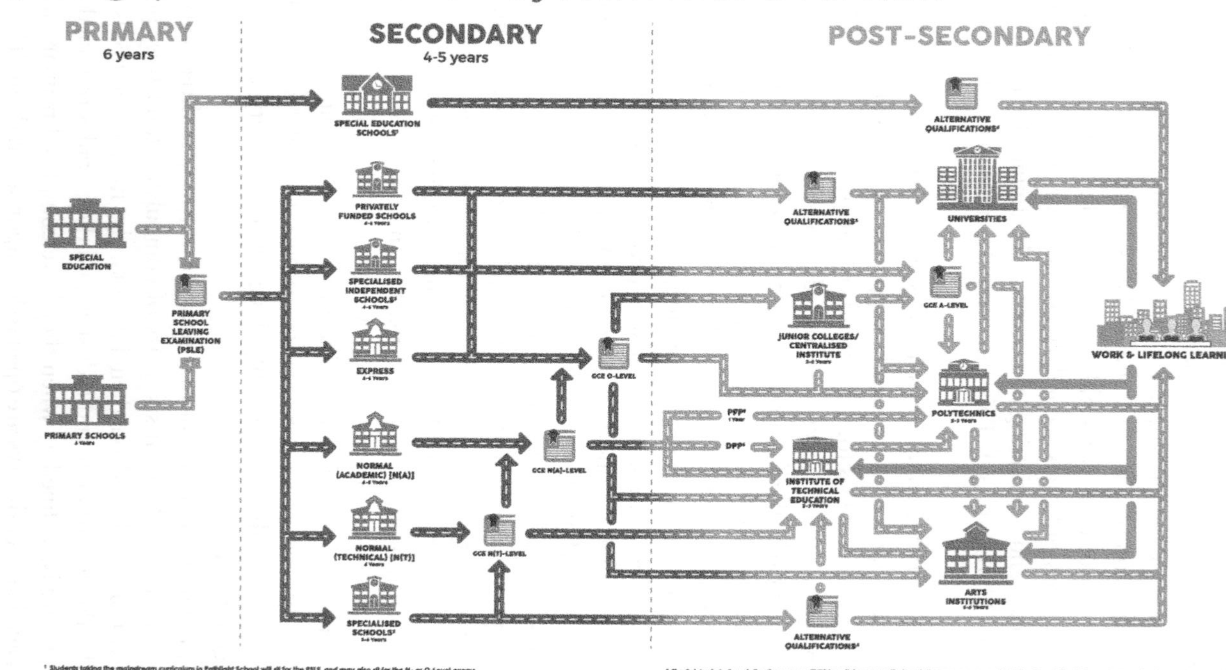

Source: MOE, https://www.moe.gov.sg/education/education-system, n.d.a.

normal technical stream. Students in both the express and normal academic streams take the General Certificate of Education: Ordinary Level (GCE O-level) examination with one difference—express stream students take the exam at the end of secondary 4, while normal academic stream students will take it at secondary 5 only if they do well in the GCE Normal (Academic) Level at secondary 4. Normal technical stream students take the GCE Normal (Technical) Level exam. The national examination system in Singapore in both the primary (i.e., the PSLE or Primary School Leaving Examination) and the secondary levels (i.e., GCE O-level, based on the British system) was put in place for academic cohort progression.

While the majority of pupils take the GCE O-levels as an intermediate benchmark of their education, there are several alternative secondary school routes open to certain students: specialized schools, the integrated program, specialized independent schools, private schools/institutions, and special schools.

Specialized schools are designed for students who are more inclined toward hands-on and practical learning. For example, schools such as Assumption Pathway and Northlight are customized for students who have not been able to pass the national examinations and who are likely to be more engaged when presented with more hands-on and practical learning pedagogies. In an effort to provide additional support to lower-achieving students, Crest Secondary School and Spectra Secondary School were established in 2013 and 2014, respectively, specifically to cater to students in the normal technical stream. The learning environments of these schools are designed to engage students via applied learning, using a whole-school approach such that the efforts permeate throughout the school and across all levels from school leaders to the teachers, right down to the administrative support staff. Additionally, the specialized schools also work closely with partners such as the ITEs (described later) in order to provide internship placements and other industrial attachment opportunities for their students.

The integrated program (IP) is designed for those pupils (13–18 years old) considered academically strong enough to engage in broader learning experiences during their secondary and postsecondary or junior college (JC) years (MOE, n.d.f.). IP provides "an integrated secondary and JC education where secondary school pupils can proceed to JC without taking the GCE O-level Examinations" (MOE, n.d.f.). In the IP, the time freed up from preparing for the GCE O-levels is used to "stretch pupils and provide greater breadth in the academic and nonacademic curriculum" (MOE, n.d.f.). Currently, there are seven integrated program schools.

The specialized independent schools offer programs designed to develop students' (13–18 years old) talents and potential in specific fields such as the arts, sports, mathematics, and the sciences. While still being government-funded, these schools have more autonomy with regard to hiring practices and curriculum design. The last alternative route in the secondary phase is private schools and institutions that offer their own customized courses for students. About 3% of local residents attend private secondary schools, whereas the vast majority attends public secondary schools.

The postsecondary phase (1–3 years) consists of six main routes. The first is junior colleges/centralized institute (grades 11–12; 2–3 years), which "prepares students for university education by equipping them with essential skills and knowledge required for tertiary education" (MOE, 2014). At this stage, students can choose subjects from different academic areas such as the humanities and the arts, languages and mathematics, and sciences; business studies are only available in the centralized institute. There are currently 25 institutions offering a pre-university curriculum—either GCE A-level (Advanced Level) curriculum or the International Baccalaureate (IB). Of these, there is 1 centralized institute, 12 are two-year junior colleges (JCs), and 12 are six-year mixed-level schools/JCs that offer the pre-university curriculum in the fifth and sixth years. A second route is the polytechnics (three years), offering a range of professional diplomas which were set up to "train middle-level professionals to support the technological and economic development of Singapore" (Teo, 2002, para. 5). Currently, there are five polytechnics.

The third postsecondary route is ITE (one to two years), whose primary role is to equip students with the technical knowledge and skills that are relevant to industry. Currently, there are three ITE colleges. Polytechnics and technical institutes are well-resourced, state-of-the-art facilities linked to contemporary labor market demands, offering strong routes to occupational mobility. As introduced in the earlier paragraph, the other three routes are integrated program, specialized independent schools, and private schools and institutions, which combine the secondary and postsecondary phases.

The university phase aims to offer an education that is "high-quality and industry-relevant" (MOE, n.d.g.). Universities are categorized into autonomous universities (e.g., National University of Singapore) and private universities (e.g., Singapore Institute of Management). Currently there are six universities in Singapore. Today, all the postsecondary routes can lead toward higher education. This is another reflection of the underlying goal of Singapore's education system—to enable everyone to realize her or his potential.

Last but not least, for students with special needs (e.g., with visual or hearing impairments/disabilities), there are special schools (3–19 years old). There are currently 20 special schools run by 13 voluntary welfare organizations, which receive funding from the Ministry of Education and the National Council of Social Service [http://ncss.org.sg/] (MOE, n.d.h.).

To ensure each and every one can benefit from the best opportunities in education, various kinds of financial assistance are provided at different levels of the education system. Primary education is provided free for all Singaporeans. Additionally, the government offers need-based financial assistance to Singapore citizens in government or government-aided schools to ensure that "all Singaporeans, regardless of their financial background, can benefit from the best opportunities in education" (MOE, n.d.e.). Subsidies are also provided for school fees to Singapore citizen students from lower and middle income families in independent schools, except for those schools (e.g., Northlight School) that have their own financial assistance plans. The financial assistance covers various expenses such as school fees, standard miscellaneous fees, textbooks, school attire, bursary, and examination fees. More affluent families also pay more for postsecondary education. Officials view this public/private partnership as garnering the resources of the wealthy in support of education, while allowing the resources of government to be channeled toward providing equitable educational access and minimizing financial barriers. Higher education is also heavily subsidized so that tuition fees are low, and need-based aid is available to make up any difference between what families can afford and the costs of a program to which students have been admitted.

For students from less-advantaged backgrounds, Singapore recognizes that beyond financial assistance, it is also important to take care of their socioemotional needs and to provide a safe and secure environment for their development. As of January 2015, there are 105 primary schools with a school-based student care center that provides additional after-school guidance and a conducive after-school environment to students who need such support. MOE will be expanding this scheme to progressively set up a student care center in all of Singapore's primary schools by the end of 2020 (Yang, 2016).

A range of differentiated instruction and programs are available to cater to students with different learning needs. There are specialized early intervention programs for lower-primary students who are at risk of having literacy and numeracy difficulties. For example, the Learning Support Programme, introduced since 1992, supports students with weaker language literacy on entry to primary (grade) 1. Specially trained teachers provide support daily to these students in small groups of 8 to 10. Similarly, the Learning Support for Mathematics is an early intervention effort aimed at providing additional support to students who do not have foundational numeracy skills and knowledge to access the primary 1 maths curriculum. Specially trained teachers work with these students for two to three additional hours a week.

Beyond the lower primary grades, there are additional learning programs targeted at supporting low progress learners, particularly in English and mathematics. Since 2013, the training of primary and secondary teachers was stepped up to equip them with teaching strategies to help students acquire numeracy skills. These teaching strategies can be used in whole class or in small group instruction, both within and outside curriculum hours. They enable students to learn at their own pace and strengthen their numeracy skills.

At this juncture, we feel it is important to introduce the teacher preparation institute that plays a crucial role in preparing the quality teachers who support the many pathways in the Singapore education system. The National Institute of Education (NIE), an autonomous institute of Nanyang Technological University (NTU), is the main and only teacher education institute for preservice teachers in Singapore. In 2015, NIE ranked 10th in the world and 2nd in Asia in the subject of education by the QS World University Rankings (Quacquarelli Symonds, 2015). As an integral part of the education system, NIE provides all levels of teacher education, ranging from initial teacher preparation, to in-service programs, graduate programs, and various courses and programs for teacher leaders, heads of departments (HODs), vice principals, and principals.

NIE began as the Teachers' Training College in 1950 and since then has been responsible for preparing practically all teachers for Singapore schools. In 1991, NIE became one of the schools housed within NTU, which is one of Singapore's five autonomous universities. Annual intake of initial teacher certification (ITC) students has been fairly consistent since 1998 at about 2,000 candidates (Goh & Lee, 2008). However, because Singapore achieved its target teaching force of about 33,000 teachers in 2012 and the system has a low teacher resignation rate of around 3%, preservice cohorts at NIE have recently been reduced to about the annual replacement rate of between 1,100 and 1,500 candidates.

Educational Governance and Policy Initiatives

According to MOE figures, just about half a million students attend 366 (MOE, 2016) primary or secondary schools and junior colleges and are taught by about 33,000 teachers. Literacy rates surpass 96% (Department of Statistics, n.d.) for residents above 15 years old and "there are opportunities for every child in Singapore to undergo at least ten years of general education" (MOE, 2013, p. vii). The majority of teachers are female (about 71%), as are the majority of principals and vice principals (MOE, 2016).

MOE plays a direct administrative role in all state schools, while for all other schools, a strong supervisory role is played, and this includes private schools. Table 1 shows the number of schools in Singapore by level and type. Of primary schools, 41 of 182 are government-aided schools; in terms of secondary schools, 28 of 154 are government-aided, 2 are independent schools, 1 is a specialized independent school and 4 are specialized schools.

In Singapore, the government-aided schools are still regarded as public schools and receive about 95% of their funding from the government. In these schools, the principal is an MOE staff member, and most of the teachers posted to the schools are MOE teachers, just like any other teacher in the public schools.

Table 1. Number of Schools by Level and Type, 2015.

Type of School	Primary	Secondary	Mixed Level[a]	Junior College/ Centralized Institute	Total
Total	182	154	16	14	366
Government	141	119	4	10	274
Government-aided	41	28	3	4	76
Independent	0	2	6	0	8
Specialized independent	0	1	3	0	4
Specialized	0	4	0	0	4

[a] The category mixed level comprises primary and secondary schools (P1-S4/5) and secondary and junior college schools (S1-JC2). For the purpose of this table, schools are reflected by type according to their secondary sections; however, their primary sections may have different classifications.

Source: MOE, 2016, p. 2.

Singapore's small size makes it easy for MOE to directly support all public schools through the 30 zonal clusters into which they are divided, and to directly develop the education service of more than 33,000 teachers and 7,700 education partners (non-education officers and allied educators). As all teachers are considered MOE employees, their professional learning and development programs are fully funded by MOE. The funding covers initial teacher preparation, beginning teacher induction, and continuing professional learning.

As the lead agency in managing the education of the nation, MOE in Singapore constantly reviews the internal and external landscape, continually obtaining feedback and inputs from the various stakeholders such as employers, parents, academics, community leaders, and students themselves, so as to prepare students for economic and social demands that are constantly shifting. Consideration is given to projecting the needs of the labor market for years into the future so that students can be well grounded in attributes that would enable them to thrive in an uncertain future. This is important because the skills that are required in the labor market evolve rather quickly; employers often remind the education system that many of today's jobs could not have been predicted 5 to 10 years ago, just as jobs in the next 5 to 10 years cannot be foreseen.

In 2007, MOE undertook a comprehensive review of the national curriculum, taking into account the future educational landscape, in an effort to crystallize the types of attributes which Singapore students ought to develop in the course of their 12-year educational journey through the school system. These attributes form the Desired Outcomes of Education (DOE[1]) (Link 2). The summary and outcomes of the review are represented in Figure 2.

The DOE[1] states that

> a person schooled in the Singapore education system should have a good sense of self-awareness, a sound moral compass, and the necessary skills and knowledge to take on challenges of the future. He/she is responsible to family, community, and nation. He/she appreciates the beauty of the world around him/her, possesses a healthy mind and body, and has a zest for life. In sum, he/she is:
>
> - a confident person who has a strong sense of right and wrong, is adaptable and resilient, knows himself/herself, is discerning in judgment, thinks independently and critically, and communicates effectively;

Figure 2. Framework for 21st-Century Competencies and Student Outcomes.

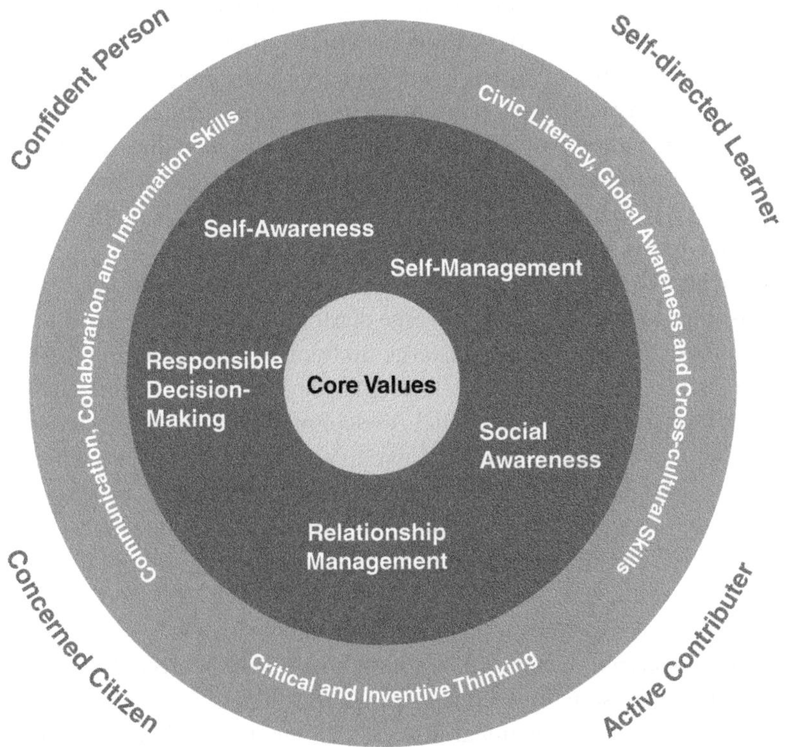

Source: MOE, n.d.i.

- a self-directed learner who takes responsibility for his/her own learning, who questions, reflects, and perseveres in the pursuit of learning;
- an active contributor who is able to work effectively in teams, exercises initiative, takes calculated risks, is innovative, and strives for excellence; and
- a concerned citizen who is rooted to Singapore, has a strong civic consciousness, is informed, and takes an active role in bettering the lives of others around him/her

Kranji Secondary School

Kranji Secondary School was one of the initial pilot schools to incorporate 21st-century competencies (21CC) and DOE into its school curriculum for the holistic development of the students. Ms. Tan Hwee Pin, the principal, noted that it was initially challenging for the school to embark on this initiative, that what was important for the effective implementation of 21CC in the school was to reduce teachers' stress levels and increase support for them. The successful implementation of 21CC in Kranji Secondary was the result of team effort and practice-based staff training. First, the school formed a core group of teachers to study the 21CC curriculum. Ms. Tan emphasized that "it is important for us to have some clarity of what 21CC is about." Therefore, the school spent a large amount of time communicating with its teachers about 21CC and sharing how these competencies might look, not just in the official curriculum but more importantly in classroom pedagogies. "It boils down to good teaching and learning," stressed Ms. Tan. The school adopted a phased approach, starting with baby steps and learning from their experiences and mistakes. The school also worked very closely with the Curriculum Planning and Development Division in MOE, which provided help and guidance on curriculum design and implementation. Exemplar lessons were collected and shared during staff training sessions—a protected time for teachers' professional learning—so that all teachers could gain a better idea of how lessons integrating 21CC might look. When it came time for teachers to come up with their own lessons, they were challenged to incorporate these competencies and bring about collaboration among the students. They were encouraged to go deeper in terms of engaging students to think critically and innovatively. Ultimately, the goal of the school is to weave 21CC into their curriculum seamlessly as an integral part of it, rather than an add-on element.

These Desired Outcomes of Education now guide the planning and design of the national curricula, cocurricular activities,[2] and the assessment model for the students. Similarly, they guide how teachers are prepared and equipped so as to be able to deliver said national curricula, cocurricular activities, and the modes of assessment, such that the Desired Outcomes of Education can be achieved. This is part of the clear vision for education we identified among the five themes. In what follows we discuss how the vision is implemented in a systemic way, supported by investments in a high-quality teaching force, assessed through developmental appraisal, and enacted and refined in Singapore's learning system.

THEME 1: A CLEAR VISION AND BELIEF IN THE CENTRALITY OF EDUCATION FOR EVERY INDIVIDUAL, THE ECONOMY, AND NATION BUILDING

Education is viewed as being central to the survival and progress of the economy and seen to be tied integrally to the larger overall goal of nation building. As a nation, Singapore is committed to helping every individual to maximize his/her full potential through education. Consequently, there is strong investment in education in terms of overall GDP spending in order to realize the vision and belief of the centrality of education for the city-state. Leaders and policymakers set the education system on future-oriented, long-term goals and effects of education. This is made possible through a very stable central government, which also believes in continuity of its policies even if specific personnel have shifted or moved on. There are also clearly articulated goals of education which are signposted to all within the system, from the policymakers, to the school leaders, teachers, parents and the students. A good example is the articulation of the 21st-century competencies (21CC) (Link 3) and the accompanying DOE. The framework for 21CC articulates student learning and development toward the skills and competencies they would require to live and work in the 21st century.

Visitors to Singapore today would be hard-pressed to believe that just 50 years ago, Singapore was a "struggling postcolonial society plagued with problems of survival," a stark contrast to the "vibrant . . . economy with a competitive edge in the world market" (Yip, Eng, & Yap, 1997, p. 4), often touted as an example for other nations. "Simply, as a small economy with little primary industry and natural resources, [Singapore] has defined its future as an information/service/digital economy driven by educational investment and development" (Luke et al., 2005, p. 8).

During the critical early years of Singapore's independence, from the mid-1960s through the mid-1970s, the constant refrain of the nation was—and remains—that her people are Singapore's "most precious resource" and that "through education every individual can realise his [*sic*] full potential, use his talents and abilities to benefit his community and nation, and lead a full and satisfying life" (MOE, n.d.a). In the immediate post-independent era, there was a severe shortage of skilled workers as very few Singaporeans had completed high school, let alone graduated from university. Fifty years later, things are quite different. In 2012, the publicly funded university cohort participation rate is 27% and the government aims to increase the rate to 40% by 2020 (MOE, 2012a). Clearly, Singapore "has skillfully used education policy to both transform society and in that process to make education a valued social institution" (Gopinathan, 2007, p. 68), thereby cementing a national belief in education as the "prime engine of economy, nation and identity" (Luke et al., 2005, p. 8).

While education has remained a bedrock value in Singapore, the focus of educational initiatives and reforms has shifted according to national imperatives and goals. Thus, the emphasis after independence from Malaysia in 1965 was "survival-driven education" (Goh & Gopinathan, 2008), aimed at achieving "universal primary education . . . and mass recruitment of teachers . . . to staff the rising number of schools" (Goh & Lee, 2008, p. 97). Teacher quality was much less a concern than recruiting sufficient numbers of teachers. The years from 1978 to 1997 saw a shift to "an efficiency-driven education," in response to Singapore's need to compete for multinational dollars and "produce skilled workers for the economy in the most efficient way" (Tan, 2005, p. 2). Quantity—enough schools with enough teachers—was now inadequate; attention was now on raising quality—upgrading schools, streaming (i.e., tracking) students according to their identified talents, designing curricula geared to students' skill levels and perceived capacities, and expanding tertiary education. "Reducing educational wastage" meant "teachers and children alike were mechanically fed by a bureaucratically designated and rigid curriculum" (Goh & Lee, 2008, p. 25).

All this changed in 1997 when then-Prime Minister (PM) Goh Chok Tong announced Thinking Schools, Learning Nation (TSLN) (Link 4), a new national vision for developing "the creative thinking skills and learning skills required for the . . . intensely global future" and making "learning a national culture" (Goh, 1997). This ushered in a focus on "ability-driven education [which] aims to identify and develop the talents and abilities of every child to the maximum" (Tan, 2005, p. 5).

Definitions of teaching and learning became more inclusive, expansive, and flexible in order to embrace diverse ways of knowing and thinking, multiple pathways and options for learning, and innovative pedagogies and technologies (Hogan & Gopinathan, 2008; Luke et al., 2005; E.H. Ng, 2008). Then-PM Mr. Goh explained in his speech:

> [Thinking Schools, Learning Nation] will redefine the role of teachers . . . Every school must be a model learning organisation. Teachers and principals will constantly look out for new ideas and practices, and continuously refresh their own knowledge. Teaching will itself be a learning profession, like any other knowledge-based profession of the future.

This impulse was further reinforced by the current PM Mr. Lee Hsien Loong in his 2004 National Day Rally speech when he urged, "We have got to teach less to our students so that they will learn more" (Lee, 2004). He emphasized the need to move away from rote learning and move toward quality/engaged learning.

The Teach Less, Learn More (TLLM) (Link 5) initiative officially introduced by MOE in 2005 was accompanied by the cultivation of a spirit of "innovation and enterprise" system-wide. This was done, in part, via the integration of technology throughout the curriculum. The paradoxical "teach less, learn more" has now become a well-known Singaporean slogan. The underpinning philosophy is to move away from the focus on content quantity to raising content quality and depth through enhancing teacher quality via providing "curriculum white space" for teachers to engage in meaningful professional development activities or professional learning communities. Then Minister of Education (in 2004) Tharman Shanmugaratnam explained the initiative from the perspective of empowering students in the learning process by allowing them to exercise their initiative to shape their own learning goals and outcomes and in so doing, to become active participants in the learning process rather than mere passive recipients of knowledge. He also urged the de-emphasis on rote-learning and emphasized the importance of teaching that caters to differences among learners and thus embraces a more holistic approach aimed at building character and life skills that can help students lead successful lives not defined merely by academic performance, but by excellence in overall character and values.

Based on the vision of TSLN and TLLM, MOE set up the Primary/Secondary/Junior College Education Review and Implementation Committee in 2008/2009 to study ways to improve the education system. In 2010, the various committees started to report their findings and recommendations for improvement.

One important recommendation was to reduce the influence exerted by examinations on teaching and the curriculum. Toward this end, the ministry began to open up admissions at all levels of the system to a wider range of indicators of student ability and talent beyond test scores, and to focus more on critical thinking and problem-solving abilities in the students.

> Syllabi, examinations and university admission criteria were changed to encourage thinking out of the box and risk-taking. Students are now more engaged in project work and higher order thinking questions to encourage creativity, independent, and inter-dependent learning. (P.T. Ng, 2008, p. 6)

For example, collaborative learning is used to enable students to work in groups and use mathematical concepts to solve scenarios drawn from real-world situations. The exchange of ideas involves students supported to engage with each other using the disciplinary discourse needed for mathematics. Students further co-create knowledge and are often asked to derive their own formulas and word problems in discussion with their classmates, after being introduced to a particular mathematical concept. As part of the quest for holistic assessments for the 21st century, Singapore has been moving toward more open-ended assessments that require critical thinking and reasoning. Upper secondary school (or high school) tests are also accompanied by tasks that can be carried out in schools via research projects, experiments, and laboratory investigations. Such school-based components, which are designed by teachers, constitute up to 20% of the examination grade. Selected projects are submitted to the university as part of the application process as well.

As stated earlier, IP schools have exempted students from the O-level examinations to reduce test-based influences on the curriculum; particularly high-achieving students may move directly to junior college without taking these tests. The goal is to "free up more time for students to experience a broader and integrated curriculum that will engage them in critical and creative thinking" (Tsuneyoshi, 2005, as cited in Darling-Hammond, 2010, p. 188).

Nice reform rhetoric, one might say, but what about the reality? When visiting schools in Singapore, research team members were able to see just how much of this vision has been actualized through the highly connected work of the ministry, its major partner for professional preparation, NIE, and the school sites. At every school visited, an emphasis on holistic education to develop well-rounded human beings was apparent. Explicit efforts to develop students cognitively, aesthetically, spiritually, morally, and socially were obvious throughout the curriculum.

In addition to project work visible in many classrooms, children were extensively involved in music, arts, calligraphy, physical education, sports, and a large variety of clubs and self-initiated activities aimed at building creativity and entrepreneurship.

Portrait of Practice

At the entrance to Ngee Ann Secondary School, which is located in the center of the Tampines housing estate (one of many publicly subsidized housing developments), there is a grand piano frequently used by students and a beautiful exhibit of professional quality student art in the open air area for all to view. Students are given opportunities to start their own little businesses in schools where any funds earned are returned to the school. In order to be granted licenses to run such businesses, they must first write a proposal and a plan. Only those whose plans have been selected are allowed to operate stalls along the school's corridors and their business licenses can be revoked, either temporarily or permanently, if they fail to adhere to the agreed rules and regulations. This novel concept thus allows students to have a foretaste of what it is like to be a mini-entrepreneur and to learn about the processes of running a business.

Principal Chua Chor Huat notes, "We try to build values and leadership in everything we do." In addition to sponsoring a student leadership group, all cocurricular activities, from the Green Movement to the debate and robotics clubs, also have student leaders. The drama club had just participated in a competition debuting a play the students wrote called "Internet Addiction," a sign of the technology-intensive lives of the students. Innovation is another theme apparent throughout the school. During physical education classes, students are asked to design innovative games and to teach them to fellow students. In Design and Technology—a course required for seventh and eighth graders that can be continued through exam-level work in ninth and tenth grades—students design and execute a range of products. A design folio for students of this school explores a theme assigned by the exam board and a wide range of design and technology issues associated with it. It includes a design for a new product with options and alternatives explored, drawings to scale, rationales for design decisions, and finally, a constructed artifact—an outdoor barbecue, a cell phone holder, or whatever meets the design challenge expectations.

Science classes also support inquiry and invention. For example, a set of students from one biology class undertook a project to create an insect repellent that is 100% organic, environmentally friendly and safe, and yet effective. They discovered that common spices such as cinnamon, cloves, and star anise have insect repellent properties and extracted oils to create an effective product in paper, liquid, and solid forms. They were among the finalists in one of the many competitions that seem to be common in every domain of life and learning in Singapore.

The TLLM initiative was accompanied by a plan for infusing technology in every school and for cultivating innovation and enterprise throughout the system in order to develop intellectual curiosity and a spirit of collective initiative. At Ngee Ann Secondary, technology infusion and collaborative learning are visible throughout the school. In a science class we observed, students worked in pairs using their laptop computers to draw a concept map of the three states of matter and the properties of each. Those who were ready moved on to map the features of kinetic particle theory, while the teacher circulated round the class to ask questions and assist. He planned to review the work that evening to identify misconceptions and understandings as the basis for the next day's lesson.

Another class of much younger students shared an inquiry they had conducted to find out, using a tachometer, what shapes of blades produce the most revolutions per minute. Their action research, presented by PowerPoint, featured careful questions and controls, and students were able to answer additional questions about how to go further in their investigation to sort out whether weight or shape was the key variable. They also explored applications of wind power for a greener approach to energy. Their teacher explained, "Action research is concerned with changing situations, not just interpreting them. . . The aim is not only to make students learn why the world works in a certain way, but rather what they can do to improve it."

Addressing the explicit effort to change the culture of right answers that has dominated in the past, the teacher also emphasized that her goal was to teach students to be comfortable in asking good questions: "Creativity and innovation may surface when there may be no clear answers, and students have to be OK working with unanswered questions."

To realize the visions of TSLN and TLLM, there is also an increasing need for assessment reform. The literature suggests that curriculum change would hardly take effect if it is not accompanied by corresponding changes in assessment. Taking into consideration the importance of changing assessment practices for improving teaching and learning, innovative reforms are also being introduced in Singapore with the aim of transforming assessment and the role it plays in education. The change is reflected both in the content and characteristics of assessments, and in how assessment information is being integrated into the learning process. For example, a new A-level curriculum and examination system was introduced in 2006 in JCs that offer grades 11 and 12. A key change introduced by the testing boards comprising the University of Cambridge Local Examinations Syndicated and the Singapore Examinations and Assessment Board (SEAB) was the introduction of performance-based assessments. These involve students in designing and conducting science investigations, engaging in collaborative project work, and completing a cross-disciplinary inquiry as part of a new subject called Knowledge and Inquiry, and allow students to draw knowledge and skills from different disciplines they have been exposed to and apply them to solving new problems or issues. Successful implementation of the proposed changes requires a shared understanding of assessment as well as public support. Therefore, to promote public acceptance of the new system, SEAB created a brochure citing positive comments from Ivy League universities in the United States and other top universities in the United Kingdom lauding such new curricular design, which is deemed to better prepare students for life and to become contributing local and global citizens.

These new assessments, like the essay and problem-based examinations they supplement, are designed by the SEAB with the help of teachers—and scored by teachers who engage in moderation processes to ensure consistency of scoring. This professional role allows teachers to better understand the standards embedded in the curriculum and to plan more effective instruction.

The emphasis on holistic education is also reflected in how schools integrate research skills as an important part of a student's academic journey. In the schools that the research team visited, we were impressed with the strong research culture that is being built—students are acquiring research skills and have become co-constructors of knowledge.  Efforts to develop students' research skills (Link 6) are fairly structured around helping students to be self-directed, critical, creative, and collaborative, as illustrated below.

Portrait of Practice

In Raffles Girls' School (RGS),[3] one of the IP schools, research is a core skill that the school aims for all students to develop; it has become an essential curriculum organizer for the students. The way that RGS hones students' research skills is rather systematic. Every discipline or subject that is offered in the school is designed so as to utilize their research skills. Right from the start of year one, students are taught through various workshops how to conduct research. In year two, they undertake a small research project. Thus, the first two years lay good ground in terms of students' research competencies. In years three and four, the students follow their interests and conduct in-depth studies on a wide array of subjects/topics in science, social science, and community projects.

To illustrate, the Humanities and Social Sciences Research Program (HSSRP) is designed for year three and year four students who are interested in and able to undertake research in the humanities and social studies. This program is jointly organized by RGS, the Gifted Education Branch at MOE, and the local universities. The students are assigned school mentors from RGS; professors and lecturers from universities who are experts in specific areas are also invited to serve as expert mentors. To participate in the program, students must first put up a proposal on a topic of interest and apply for approval. Once their proposals are accepted by the expert mentors from the universities, students can commence with their projects. The matching of expert mentors and students is done by the MOE Gifted Education Branch, which means that the mentors also have a deep interest in the topics that students have proposed. Some of the topics include "the correlation between speakers' mother tongue capability versus their cultural pride," "the high cost of preschool education in Singapore and how low income families are coping with it," and "what are the benefits for Singapore in terms of its support for the US war efforts in Vietnam between 1965 and 1975."

To guide the students to successfully complete their projects, comprehensive support is given to them. For instance, the school mentor consults students weekly to give them guidance and to: (1) motivate them and help them maintain their research interest; (2) facilitate students' communications with their expert mentors; (3) vet students' work/reports before they are sent to the expert mentors; (4) help them tackle their problems in terms of how to formulate research questions, analyze data, source for information. Besides the consultation hour, the school mentor also accompanies students during field work if necessary. The expert mentor provides expertise in the field/topic that students are pursuing. He/she helps the students by directing them to information sources, guiding them on the literature review, and vetting their reports. Expert mentors also make sure the student's report is of sufficient quality for publication at the end of the HSSRP.

The current paradigm framing educational practice and innovation in Singapore emphasizes "a student-centric, values-driven education" (Link 7) which rests on the "core belief that every child can learn—not just in school but for the rest of his (*sic*) life" (Heng, 2012). The shift from identifying specific ability in some, to nurturing and enhancing capacity among all learners, "regardless of background or ability" (Heng, 2012), requires a corresponding shift across the educational enterprise. Teachers, schools, and parents are now being called upon to fully participate in ensuring that "every student [is] an engaged learner" (Heng, 2012). This conception of learning and teaching currently driving educational reform and innovation indicates that Singapore has reached a level of success that now allows her the luxury (and necessity) of thinking beyond basic education to consider the deeper and more complex questions of quality and equality as they are jointly pursued in the Singapore context. Thus, educational reforms sparked by TSLN focused attention on teachers and fueled significant changes in teacher recruitment, preparation, compensation, status, and professional development, changes that have had an indelible impact on teacher quality and the teaching profession in Singapore, an impact that continues to be felt today. This moves us nicely to our second theme to be covered in the next section.

THEME 2: A SYSTEMIC APPROACH TO INNOVATION, REFORM, AND CHANGE

The Singapore Education system can be regarded as one which is coherently managed such that there is alignment among the different components that make up the system. The system can be encapsulated by the PPP model, which stands for the Policies-Practice-Preparation model. This is represented by the illustration in Figure 3. The Teacher Preparation Model that NIE adopts in preparing teachers for the whole education system is underpinned by this philosophy of coherence and alignment.

Figure 3. The Policies-Practice-Preparation (PPP) Model for the Management of an Education System.

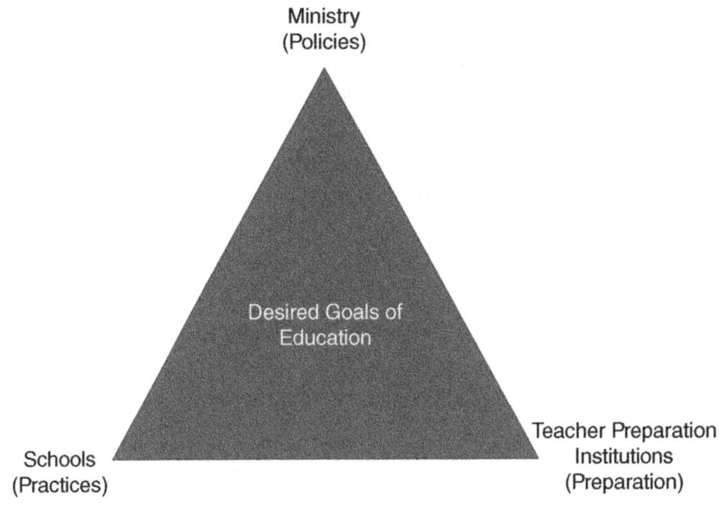

Source: Lee & Low, 2014a.

How does this model work? An education system must have clear goals of education so that there are clear parameters of attainment at the end of a period of learning. The "players" within the system must be in sync so that there is alignment of work, as this will enable the goals of education to be impactfully achieved. This systemic approach acknowledges that there are three key players, each with a specific role to fulfill. There are other players as well, such as parents, teachers associations, and local community members, but this articulation is limited to those within the system itself: the ministry, the schools, and the teacher preparation institution.

Ministry or Lead Agency of Education: In order to craft a systemic approach, MOE must provide leadership by conducting comprehensive reviews of the broader landscape (social, civic, economic, etc.), such that the goals of education established are relevant to the time and the needs of the landscape, and students are well grounded so as to be similarly relevant within the landscape. Having established the relevant goals of education, the lead agency must then develop *policies* to enable the goals of education to be achieved. These policies, including the national curricula, assessment philosophy, HR policies for teachers and school leaders, etc., should take into consideration input from professionals, the practitioners, and the stakeholders in order to ensure that they are well received and will support attainment of the goals of education.

Besides the formulation of goals and policies, the Singapore MOE has two other critical roles that can make a lot of difference in policy implementation. The first is the role in resourcing schools to deliver its policies, such as funding physical infrastructure (e.g., laboratories, IT), people (e.g., senior specialists and master teachers who support schools in curriculum implementation), and materials (e.g., approved textbooks, ICT learning resources). Therefore, there is less disjuncture between policies and the resources required to deliver them. The second is the role of putting in place structures and procedures to ensure fidelity of implementation of policies and initiatives across all schools, with the aim of leveling up all schools. Examples of such structures and mechanisms include the cluster system and the school excellence model of self-appraisal.

Teacher Preparation Institute: To effectively translate policies into practices, school leaders and teachers are essential. School leaders and teachers must be well prepared with the appropriate values, skills, and knowledge that will enable them to develop the practices needed to deliver the national curricula and adopt the appropriate assessment processes in order to achieve the goals of education. The teacher preparation institution must therefore translate the policies into relevant teacher *preparation* programs so that both the school leaders and teachers are appropriately equipped for the tasks in the schools. The PPP model ensures alignment, hence the impact in achieving educational goals.

Schools: Schools are the key in enabling the goals of educations to be achieved. The schools must translate the policies into appropriate *practices* so that students are educated through a series of programs and subjects based on the national curricula such that the goals of education are attained. This would involve the pedagogies adopted, the design of the learning environment, and the assessment processes. Other cocurricular activities can also be planned and implemented to ensure the attainment of values and character building.

Central to the attainment of the educational goals is the quality of teachers and teaching. As a system, Singapore takes recruitment, preparation, and professional development of its teachers very seriously. Teachers are hired by MOE, and the size of the teaching force has grown progressively from 24,600 in 2001 to 33,000 today. In the last two years, recruitment has fallen to between 1,100 and 1,400, down from the peak of recruitment in 2009 when the numbers reached 3,000 (Davie, 2014). Rather than an across-the-board reduction in class size, the growth in the overall teaching workforce allows more customized teaching to meet the needs of students, such as better support for struggling students, more subject combinations, greater flexibility between courses and streams, additional cocurricular activities, and enrichment programs (Heng, 2012; MOE, 2011).

The ministry continually engages in strategic planning in terms of forecasting the numbers of teachers needed in the future—resulting from forces of natural attrition such as retirements or resignations, to future systemic needs such as the overall numbers needed in the workforce or forecasting growth areas in specific disciplines requiring more teachers. This careful balancing of the number of teachers that Singapore needs and the preparation required for their entry and success into the profession and schools is at the heart of the ministry-schools-teacher preparation institute partnership, which focuses simultaneously on quantity, quality, and innovation.

What we see then is that the PPP model provides a structure to help ensure that ideas and actions are tightly coupled, and that adequate resources are strategically deployed to support deliberate movement from conception to enactment. However, it is not the model per se that enables systemic innovation and change for managing education systems but the dynamism of the model that brings the three Ps into action, such that each P has a part to play, but that part is in relationship to or in concert with the others. One example is the recent policy focus on teacher development, continued learning, and teacher leadership. This focus emerged from forecasting—on the part of MOE—of the need for advanced teacher preparation given a teaching force that had attained a certain size and level of education (as mentioned earlier). Given low levels of attrition, with most teachers at a fairly early stage in their careers, it became important to shift attention from recruitment and preparation, to retention and advancement, and to think about different mechanisms for sustaining in-service teachers by nurturing their leadership aspirations and capabilities, and igniting them as lifelong learners.

MOE has established an Academy of Singapore Teachers (AST) and other academies and language centers to provide teacher-led professional development for teachers. These academies and language centers work with teachers and connect to schools to provide professional opportunities "by teachers for teachers" through the extensive networks of teacher leaders who offer a wide range of professional learning courses, activities, learning communities, resources, and expertise. In turn, schools have created spaces for learning and sharing among teachers, by building into the timetable dedicated periods for teachers to engage in professional learning communities, and for senior teachers to support their peers. The various types of professional communities that work together to hone practice and design the learning environment have been a great enabler in helping schools to attain the goals of education. Under the PPP model, teacher professional learning not only takes place within the teacher preparation institute, but is also rather continuous across the system, and occurs within various levels of teacher communities which are led by teachers. For example, there is a strong culture of mentoring of teachers within schools, as shown in international studies such as the Teaching and Learning International Survey (TALIS) (OECD, 2014b). Professional learning in teams and communities allows teachers to focus on shared goals, develop appropriate action plans, and improve practices collectively. Finally, NIE—the preparation institute—works in collaboration with MOE to conduct several teacher leadership programs that are designed to support the professional learning aims of MOE for in-service teachers. This synergy among the schools, the ministry, and NIE ensures that ideas come to fruition quickly, that all partners are working simultaneously on new initiatives and change, and that the efforts of each are interconnected and mutually supporting.

We turn now to this most crucial aspect of the Singapore case study to describe in detail what it means to recruit, prepare, sustain, and retain strong teachers in this particular context. The discussion is anchored by themes three to five of our case study: (3) a high-quality teaching force—recruiting and preparing; (4) educative and developmental appraisal—nurturing and retaining; and (5) a learning system and a learning profession—retaining and sustaining. We begin with a description of how Singapore attracts strong and well-qualified candidates and prepares them to instruct the nation's most precious resource.

THEME 3: INVESTING IN A HIGH-QUALITY TEACHING FORCE

Recruiting Quality

With evidence pointing to the fact that teacher quality is one of the most important in-school factors influencing student achievement (Chetty, Friedman, & Rockoff, 2013; Darling-Hammond, 2000; Hattie, 2003), the focus on raising teacher quality has gained worldwide attention (Buchberger, Campos, Kallos, & Stephenson, 2000; International Alliance of Leading Education Institutes, 2008; International Reading Association, 2008). In Singapore, the explicit goal of teacher education, in which the government invests heavily, is to produce high-quality teachers.

Teaching is a highly attractive profession in Singapore. Important policies and measures that have contributed hugely to its attractiveness include sponsored tuition and additional stipends for preservice preparation, secured positions at schools after graduating from preservice preparation, competitive salaries, and career ladders that suit teachers' diversified aspirations. In addition, teaching as a whole enjoys high social status and respect from the public.

MOE takes specific actions to recruit the best teachers into service. It puts up advertisements in various media and platforms to "sell" teaching as an attractive career; marketing and publicity strategies focus on informing prospective candidates about the value of the teaching profession and the many professional opportunities in education. MOE selects from the top one-third of each cohort—defined as each annual entering primary 1 (grade 1 equivalent) cohort—underscoring the long-term view of teacher quality taken in Singapore. With a highly selective application process, approximately one out of three shortlisted applicants makes it through the selection interview.

According to a study conducted by McKinsey and Company (2007), Singapore's teacher recruitment process is one of the most effective among top performing systems. From their interview data with MOE,

Figure 4. The Process of Teacher Recruitment in Singapore.

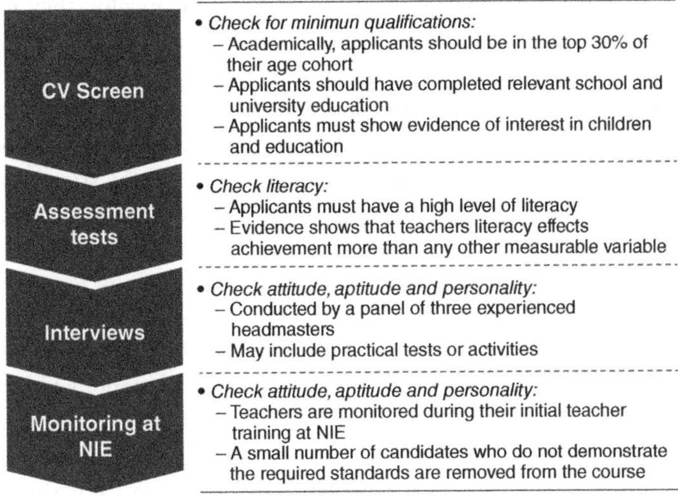

Source: McKinsey & Company, 2007, p. 17.

McKinsey and Company (2007) summarized the recruitment process in Singapore in Figure 4. Grounded in the systemic approach described earlier, teacher recruitment in Singapore is a single, statewide selection process, jointly managed by MOE and NIE. It places emphasis on candidates' academic achievement, communications skills, and motivation for joining the profession and relies on school partners to be key decision-makers in the selection process.

The position that individuals apply for is named as an untrained teaching position. Applicants will first have to get to know the various teacher education programs available and decide on the route they would like to pursue. These programs, all of them offered by NIE, can be categorized according to each applicant's academic qualification. They are the 16-month Postgraduate Diploma in Education (PGDE) and the two-year PGDE (physical education) for degree holders; the Bachelor of Arts (BA)/Bachelor of Science (Education) (Link 8); Diploma in Education for A-level/diploma holders, and for O-level holders (Link 9); Teacher Training Schemes for Tamil, Art, Music and Chinese (Link 10). Whether a candidate qualifies for the four-year degree program or the two-year diploma program is largely determined by their A-level or polytechnic

diploma results. When individuals have decided on the program that they would like to pursue, they submit their application via the MOE Teach website. Applicants' CVs are strictly screened according to the standards listed in the first step of Figure 4. Academically, they must be in the top 30% of their age cohort and should have completed relevant secondary and/or university education. They must also show passion for education and teaching. As will be introduced later on in this section, an important way to assess teacher candidates' motivation and passion for teaching is the introduction of a compulsory teaching stint in schools if possible before their formal enrollment in teacher preparation. This policy applies to candidates applying for the PGDE programs.

Apart from meeting the basic academic qualifications for entry into the programs, applicants are required to sit and pass relevant Entrance Proficiency Tests. For example, if their language performance at the O- or A-levels does not meet the minimum required standards for selection, as indicated in Step 2 of Figure 4, they will be required to take a language proficiency test. Research suggests that literacy affects achievement (Bilton, 1977; Lee, 1997). Of particular importance is the English proficiency of the candidates, which is a key requirement of the initial teacher preparation (ITP) programs at NIE (Low, 2014). Low (2014) observes that Singapore's English language policy and language teacher education have contributed significantly to the sustained high achievement of Singapore students in internationally benchmarked tests. For example, PISA results show that Singaporean students who speak English at home performed on average 58 points higher than those who speak another language at home (OECD, 2010). This result further underlies the importance of English language literacy of teacher candidates (Low, 2014). For both its degree programs and PGDE program, NIE requires a minimum qualification of English (e.g., General Certificate of Education: Ordinary). To qualify for an exemption, candidates must have performed well enough in previous milestone examinations. Candidates who choose to teach mother tongue languages (Chinese, Malay, or Tamil) do not have to take the same English language proficiency test. However, if they wish to teach an English-medium subject in the future, they must take the additional English Language Entrance Proficiency Test (Low, 2014). It should be noted that proficiency tests are not just limited to English. For example, teacher candidates who wish to teach physical education, art, or music must undergo an NIE-conducted Physical Proficiency Test, art interview, or music interview, respectively. For candidates applying to teach mother tongue languages, MOE will, at its discretion, require them to sit for the mother tongue entrance proficiency tests.

Academic qualifications form the basis for shortlisting potential teacher candidates for interview. At the shortlist stage, teachers must demonstrate the aptitude for and interest in the profession to a panel chaired by a currently serving or recently retired principal or vice principal (Teo, 2000, cited in Ingersoll, 2007). Attributes that interview panelists are seeking include good communication skills, deep passion for teaching, and potential to be a good role model to their future students. According to Sclafani and Lim (2008, p. 3),

> the Ministry is looking for and finding those young people who have a passion for helping others. Community service is part of every student's education in Singapore, and assignments of working with younger students or peers who need tutors help teachers identify students who should be encouraged to be teachers.

MOE requires applicants to the PGDE program to go through a compulsory school stint, during which they will be hired as an untrained contract teacher. The school stint is centrally organized by MOE before these applicants enter ITP at NIE. Its purpose is to enable the school to assess the applicant's suitability for teaching and the applicant to affirm her or his interest and passion for the profession. It is also to allow applicants to experience the life of a teacher and relate their future learning at NIE to their firsthand experience. There are two types of school stint—contract teaching and enhanced school experience (ESE). Generally, the length of contract teaching may range from a few months to a year; the length of ESE is four weeks. ESE provides student teachers opportunities to know the school culture and environment, observe experienced teachers and co-teach, and have structured reflections on these experiences (NIE, 2009). Contract teaching differs from ESE in that it has a longer duration and usually involves an extended period of co-teaching/teaching experience.

Before PGDE candidates go for their school stint, they are required to attend the Introduction to Teaching Programme run by AST, which is an introductory course that provides all contract untrained teachers with an awareness of the expectations and ethos of the profession, and the fundamentals of teaching. These would include adopting a growth mindset, lesson planning and enactment, assessment for learning, and classroom management. Components like ICT infusion and character and citizenship education are also included. In school, the contract teachers take on full teaching duties similar to trained teachers and assist with department work and cocurricular activities. However, they are not required to set examination or test papers. To make sure that they do not undermine students' learning, all their professional activities in schools are under the guidance and supervision of their school mentor (usually a more experienced teacher or a teacher leader) and their reporting officer (usually the head of department or subject head).

If the candidate is assessed by the school as being suitable for teaching at the end of their school stint, and he/she remains committed to pursuing this profession, she/he will be enrolled in NIE to undergo ITP. However, it must be noted that candidates will continue to be monitored at NIE while they undergo their ITP (step 4 in Figure 4). Candidates who do not meet the requirements on attitude, aptitude, and personality will be removed from the program—typically a small number. Starting from the school stint before entering preservice education, candidates receive a full monthly salary from MOE. Candidates who are mid-career professionals receive starting salaries that recognize their previous working experience. Teacher candidates not only receive free preservice training but also receive a stipend/salary while training. The salary range for students in the Diploma in Education (Dip Ed) programs is from S$1,480 to S$2,550 monthly. Undergraduates in the BA/BSc (Ed) programs programs will receive salaries similar to the Dip Ed candidates in the first two years. At year 3 and year 4, eligible candidates[4] who have done exceptionally well in the first two years will qualify for the MOE salary of S$5,000 per year in year 3 and year 4, if they continue to perform well throughout their undergraduate study. Candidates in the PGDE will receive a salary from S$2,000 to S$4,340 (NIE, 2014).

Once potential teacher candidates have cleared the selection interview and signed the training deed with MOE, they are appointed as general education officers and will receive the following while they are in their training program preparing to teach: a monthly salary for up to two years according to MOE pay scales and criteria; benefits (such as medical copay insurance coverage); an annual 13-month bonus (given to all Singapore civil servants on permanent establishment); a variable bonus depending on the economic health of the country, and other bonuses tied to performance or other relevant work experiences. All student teachers' tuition fees are fully covered by MOE, and they are provided funds to purchase materials such as books and laptop computers. Upon graduation, new teachers have to complete a bond of service of between three and four years, depending on whether they attended the graduate or undergraduate program of study. When they enter teaching, they earn a competitive starting salary comparable to those of beginning accountants and engineers. This translates to a starting monthly salary of about S$3,010–S$3,310 for degree holders.

As Sclafani and Lim (2008, p. 3) point out:

> How does Singapore get high-performing students to apply? It is not just future salary, although salaries are competitive with those of engineers in the civil service. It is a combination of factors. The most immediate is that the Ministry pays all tuition, fees and a monthly stipend to undergraduate teaching candidates. For those who enter teacher preparation at the graduate level, the stipend is equivalent to what they would have made as college graduates in a civil sector job. Since this must be repaid if the candidate fails the program or leaves the profession before the stipulated period. . . it is also a powerful motivator for serious commitment to the program.

One of the highlights of teacher recruitment in Singapore is the wide array of attractive teaching scholarships and awards offered by MOE and the Public Service Commission. Each year, around 300 scholarships and awards are offered by MOE. These scholarships are a long-term recruitment scheme for potential teacher candidates. They target students who are obtaining their postsecondary qualifications (e.g., A-level, international baccalaureate [IB], polytechnic diploma) and year 1–3 undergraduates pursuing courses in the local universities. Successful applicants are sent to study at top universities around the world, including the prestigious local universities. MOE not only covers the tuition fees when students undertake their regular degrees, but also their PGDE teacher training fees when they come to NIE (these scholars will need to attend the PGDE programs at NIE after they graduate from their undergraduate studies). The scholarship holders are considered to have great potential and are given various kinds of additional opportunities and exposure including MOE headquarters attachments that involve challenging policy projects to better prepare them for a career at MOE in the future, school attachments that afford firsthand teaching experience, and challenging school projects to stretch their capabilities, overseas attachments to foreign educational institutions to get a glimpse of how education systems and schools function in other countries and their differences from Singapore's system (as well as possible opportunities to teach while on attachment), exposure to policy making through attending the Developments in Public Policy Seminar and learning journeys to better understand the rationale behind certain policies, and dialog sessions with MOE's top policymakers expose them to broader policy and strategic considerations guiding education policy (MOE, n.d.d.).

Most recently in 2014, MOE introduced the premier NTU-NIE Teaching Scholars Program (TSP) to encourage the best and brightest of the A-level and polytechnic students to pursue the four-year BA/BSc (Ed) programs at NIE. The program aims to "prepare tomorrow's leaders of education who possess the passion and aspiration to inspire, nurture, and lead our next generation" (NIE, n.d.c). The curriculum of TSP is greatly enhanced through a series of measures including electives for TSP participants to engage in critical discussions with other NTU scholars, the opportunity to expand their skills by taking up a minor program among more than 30 choices in NTU, opportunities to conduct cutting-edge research under the tutelage of eminent researchers and top professors through NTU's Undergraduate Research Experience on Campus, exposure to experiential learning, and overseas immersion. These enhancements aim to ensure that TSP scholars will "acquire essential knowledge, practical experience, and absolute confidence to embark on a successful career in education" (NIE, n.d.c.).

Perceptions of Teaching as a Career

Still, financial incentives aside, altruistic motivations for entering teaching remain powerful. In a 2011 study, Low, Lim, Ch'ng, and Goh investigated preservice teachers' reasons for choosing teaching as a career in Singapore across three different ITP programs in Singapore. With over 1046 responses, the study showed that young people's motivation for entering teaching may be divided into altruistic, intrinsic, and extrinsic reasons, with the majority being motivated by intrinsic, followed by altruistic, and then extrinsic reasons (see Table 2). The reason most cited by the preservice teachers is "interest in teaching."

Preservice students interviewed talked extensively about the intangible rewards of teaching (Lortie, 1975), reiterating much of what is said by the extant literature on teaching—teaching to make a difference, teaching to care for young people, teaching as a calling. Candidates spoke of their disappointment in other professions, such as the finance industry where they found "actually not much meaning there." This led one interviewee to try out contract teaching and the subsequent discovery that teaching was "actually something I enjoy, I find it meaningful to make a difference in a student's life." Another talked about "realising that the connection between human and human is much more meaningful and I like this kind of thing compared to banking." The fact that teachers are actually inculcating some values in students' lives came across as a strong draw to teaching for many interviewees.

Table 2. Main Reason for Choosing to Join the Teaching Profession (n = 1064).

Category	Reason	Frequency	Percentage (%)
Altruistic	Love of children/young people	208	19.5
	To fulfill a mission	209	19.6
	To answer a calling	19	1.8
Intrinsic	Interest in teaching	267	25.1
	Job factor or fit	216	20.3
	Inspired by role models	55	5.2
	For the love of the subject	42	3.9
Extrinsic	Financial reasons	22	2.1
	Teaching as a stepping stone	12	1.1
Others	Others	11	1.0
	No response	3	0.3
Total		1064	99.9

Source: Low et al. 2011, p. 203.

Other interviews of teacher candidates indicated their desire to emulate or recreate their own positive school experiences. They reflected on their own teachers who "influenced my life. So I think I'm quite privileged that both for primary and secondary school I had teachers, good teachers" and talked about wanting "to care for students, how my teacher cared for me as in, they were very positive." These personal experiences, while not uniformly positive—"definitely I had my share of good teachers, bad teachers"—apparently engendered in some prospective teachers "that desire, as a student, to make things better in the future for others, for the future students."

Finally, interviewees also talked about the ultimate intrinsic motivation to teach—teaching as a calling. For some, teaching "was just. . .it was just something that I always knew that I wanted to do." For example, one candidate described a desire to teach that went back to "Since I was in primary 3, I think I have always wanted to become a teacher"; another began thinking about teaching "definitely at the end of JC, education was, I wouldn't say a very obvious choice but I definitely felt like there was something I could do in this field."

Teaching has always depended heavily on entrants' altruistic motivations—the possibility of doing meaningful work that could make a difference in the lives of young people is a draw whose force cannot be minimized. However, a common international trend is that economic realities often mean some prospective teachers turn to other professions that offer better remuneration and the possibility of affording a comfortable life style, or they leave the profession because they find that the psychic rewards coupled with the challenges presented by teaching cannot outweigh the lack of compensation or support (Hutchings, 2011). Thus, financial incentives to teach are important and in fact allow those considering teaching to focus on the profession and on their professional goals, and not on whether they can make a living wage.

Professional Perspective

Mr. Azahar Bin Mohd Noor, the teacher we interviewed at RGS, reflected upon how his perception of teaching as a feasible choice changed as a result of the government's effort to increase teachers' pay and boost the status of the profession:

> In the past, I was reluctant to join teaching, because I felt that we sometimes equate remuneration with status. But at least in the last 10 years, teachers are very well paid. With that, I think the status of teaching and teachers have gone up not only in terms of money, but also in terms of professionalism. I think today, we can really call ourselves professionals, not just workers. We know that we are professionals.

He elaborated on the concept of professionalism:

> Professionalism is not just about content mastery, but also about mastery in our pedagogy and being competent as a classroom teacher, which builds our professional identity. I don't see myself as any smaller or any lower than a lecturer or other academics in a university because my specialty is really about pedagogy and I'm dealing with young learners.

Based on the feedback we receive from many other teachers, principals, HODs, and senior teachers, the view that teaching is high status seems to be a common perception of the teaching fraternity. The high status of teaching is not only the result of governmental efforts in terms of its policies but also stems from the general views on education and teachers.

Professional Perspective

Mrs. Mary Cheriyan, the director of the Centre for Pedagogical Research and Learning (PeRL) at RGS, stressed that "In Singapore, because we pay such a premium on education, educators tend to be respected." Mrs. Poh Mun See, the principal of RGS, considers teachers as a very fortunate group of people in Singapore, because much importance is attached to education by parents, students, and members of the public. She also attributed the high prestige that teachers enjoy to the government's continuing strong supply of resources to recruit, develop, and sustain teachers in the system.

Ms. Tan Hwee Pin, the principal of Kranji Secondary School, contends that the reputation of teaching as a career has changed over the years. She relates how her teacher colleagues have changed their views regarding their own children's career choices. She recalled that

> I had colleagues who used to say that they would discourage their children to go into teaching because it was such a tough job—they wanted their children to pursue other careers. However, in recent years, I don't hear that anymore; they support their children's teaching aspirations and even encourage them to take up teaching awards. I am extremely heartened when I hear that.

The quantitative findings on teachers' perceptions of the teaching profession from TALIS (OECD, 2014b) corroborate our qualitative evidence. It was found that most teachers (88%) in Singapore are satisfied with their job. Given the choice to decide again, 82% of teachers in Singapore would still choose to enter teaching (TALIS average = 78%). In addition, 68% of teachers believe that the teaching profession is valued in the Singapore society, way above the TALIS average of 31%.

As part of the effort to further strengthen the teaching profession, the ministry aimed to have an all-graduate teaching workforce by 2015. Currently, the stand is that in-service teachers who do not possess a degree but have proven themselves through a good track record will be remunerated as well as their graduate peers.

Teacher Distribution across Schools

MOE not only organizes all recruitment efforts but also recruits according to vacancies in schools and in response to shortages in specific subject areas. School postings are also determined by the ministry depending on manpower needs. Thus, successful applicants to teacher preparation are not only salaried during their preparation but are also assured of employment upon program completion. At the same time, schools are assured of new teachers who are well prepared and have been specifically selected to meet their needs. There is an open posting exercise centrally administered by the ministry on an annual basis for all teachers after they have completed at least two years of service in their first placement. Principals are free to identify suitable candidates for their schools but must first seek the consent of principals of the schools where teachers are currently serving.

Teacher resignation rates in Singapore are low by international standards of around 3%. MOE found that teachers' top three reasons for staying in the profession include a positive professional culture, good remuneration that is competitively benchmarked, and ample opportunities for professional development and career growth.

However, in keeping with growing flexibility in the system, the human resource (HR) processes and systems in independent schools are quite different from government schools. This flexibility enables independent schools to enact their specific mission and meet the unique needs of the students they serve. Recruitment into independent schools is done directly by the principals of these schools, who have the freedom of selecting graduates from NIE or with other qualifications. However, when found, suitable candidates without NIE qualifications are sent to NIE for their preservice teacher education program. For example, Mrs. Poh Mun See, the principal of RGS, told us:

> As an independent school, we have our own HR processes and systems, which are quite different from mainstream schools. We are very student-centered in the way we design our programs for our students. First, we look at the kind of students we have. In the case of RGS, we have high ability students—girls who are very gifted and talented. We design the programs centered on their needs. Then from the programs we decide the kind of teachers and staff we need in order to deliver those programs. We don't require a teaching qualification when they apply, although we do try to look for people with teaching qualification and preferably from NIE. But we also consider applicants without that qualification. We will still hire them and if we find them

> suitable to continue teaching in the school, we will send them to NIE and pay for their course.

However, the principal emphasized that the expectations and qualities for RGS teachers are different from the mainstream schools due to the unique profile of the students in the school. Thus applicants to RGS must understand "we are a school of gifted and talented students. When people come to apply, we always tell them that in RGS we adopt the gifted and talented education model." RGS programs are also unique because "we are a girls' school, certain programs are run catering to the girls. . .[and]. . . the purpose of all our programs and activities is to develop the gifted and talented girl." A final area that is made explicit to applicants is the kind of pedagogy that the school would like to see in its teachers. With high-ability students, the pace of learning is often accelerated. "The girls are talented and they learn very fast. All the content you have prepared may already be known to them when you go to class. How do you make things interesting to them?" This means teachers must be skilled at planning lessons that are interesting, engaging, and challenging enough to stretch the girls.

Preparing Quality

> Except for teachers in independent schools, all potential teachers are required to complete a university-based program offered by NIE before they can join schools as fully qualified teachers. The adoption of the university-based model demonstrates that teaching is a profession, where the development of teachers is underpinned by evidenced-based learning, and where teachers require the award of a degree as a pre-requisite for joining the profession.
>
> (NIE, 2009, p. 22)

Teacher education at NIE is guided by the Teacher Education Model for the 21st Century (TE^{21}). TE^{21} aims to prepare teachers for a much more heterogeneous student population, who are named the EPIIC learners (Tan & Liu, 2014). EPIIC learners require *Experiential* and *Participatory* learning and strongly need *Imagery*, *Inquiry*, and *Connectivity*. It also means preparing teachers to be autonomous thinking professionals who can perform the multiple roles of 21st century teaching such as knowledge organizer, motivator, facilitator, co-inquirer, facilitator, and designer of the learning processes (Darling-Hammond, 2006; Tan, Liu, & Low, 2012; Tan & Liu, 2014). The goal of teaching can no longer be the transmission of knowledge; it is no longer sufficient to merely prepare teachers to deliver a standardized curriculum (Darling-Hammond, 2006).

TE[21] reflects NIE's effort to stay relevant and responsive to the increasingly complex nature of teaching and the formidable goal of developing the whole child (NIE, 2009; Tan & Liu, 2014). Therefore, ITP now aligns with the nation's new vision of teaching and learning that is "student-centric, values-driven" (Heng, 2012) and embodies the aim of TE[21] to prepare "*autonomous thinking teachers* for the 21st century through *a new paradigm of teacher education*, supported by *a robust partnership with stakeholders* and *a strong theory practice link in the programs*" (Tan & Liu, 2014, p. 140, italics in original). This is evident in NIE's V³SK framework for teacher preparation:

> NIE's initial teacher preparation is one that is very strongly pivoted on a three-pronged set of values (V) with skills (S) and knowledge (K) needed of a 21st Century Teaching professional wrapped around the central pillar of values. . . Key to [the V³SK framework] is a clear reiteration of NIE's belief that the learner is the centre of our teacher education mission. This framework is premised along three value paradigms: learner-centredness, teacher identity, and service to the profession and the community. . .[T]he skills and knowledge spelt out in this framework refer to key skills and knowledge competencies that 21st century teaching professionals require in order to bring about 21st century literacies and learning outcomes (see Figure 5). These skills and competencies are closely aligned with the Ministry of Education's articulation of desired student outcomes as outlined in their Curriculum 2015 (C2015) document (NIE, n.d.e).

As the framework that undergirds all the ITP programs, whether graduate or undergraduate, V³SK has resulted in programmatic changes and the development of new processes, structures, or assessments. The three central values pillars of TE[21] are "emphasised consistently, holistically, and methodologically throughout the programs" (Tan & Liu, 2014, p. 143). The first value paradigm, *learner-centered values*, puts the learner at the core of the teacher's work. NIE's programs emphasize that teachers ought to have a deep understanding of learners' development and diversity and be committed to bringing out the fullest potential of each child. For example, in the educational psychology courses, preservice teachers are introduced to important concepts about learners and learning and required to reflect on how these theories can be used to maximize learning for different learners. Such reflections aim to strengthen their beliefs that every child can learn (Lee & Low, 2014b). In practicum,

Figure 5. The V³SK Framework from NIE.

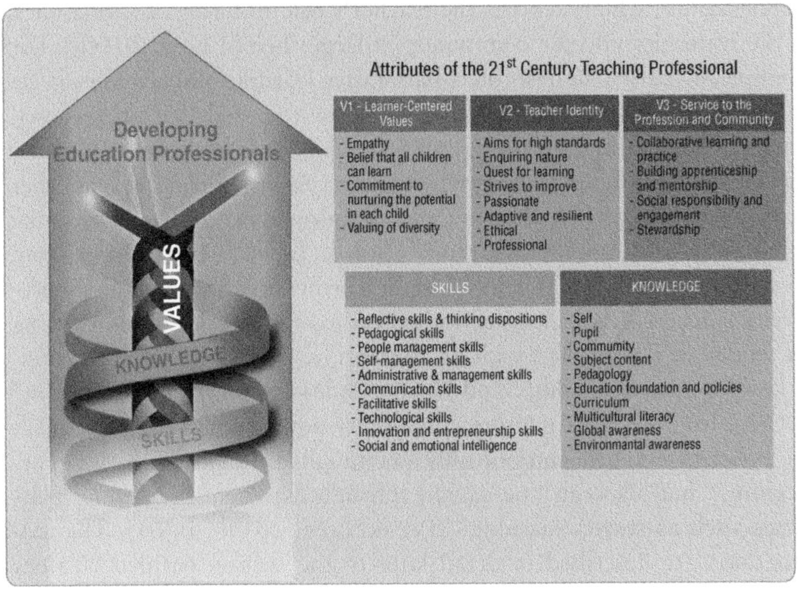

Source: NIE, 2012, p. 6.

for example, they are asked to reflect on how teaching can facilitate or impede the learning of diverse learners (Tan & Liu, 2014).

The second value paradigm is *teacher identity*, which aims to facilitate preservice teachers' development of a strong sense of professional identity. It refers to "the core beliefs a teacher has about teaching and being a teacher" (Tan & Liu, 2014, p. 144). Research has shown that teachers who have developed a strong teacher identity will stay longer and contribute more effectively to the profession (e.g., Day, Kington, Stobart, & Sammons, 2006; Gu & Day, 2007). Teachers with a strong professional identity uphold the professionalism, integrity, and values of the teaching fraternity (Lee & Low, 2014b). They are passionate about their subject and their role as a teacher, and have a deep drive for high standards. They have a thirst for learning and an inquisitive nature. They are ethical, adaptable, and resilient in the challenging educational landscape. In NIE's programs, focused conversations serve as one of the platforms where preservice teachers share and articulate their core beliefs about education, teaching, and learning, which can in turn help them crystallize their professional identity (Tan & Liu, 2014).

The third value paradigm is *service to the profession and community*. It focuses on stewardship, mentoring, collaborative learning, and social responsibility, which denotes the teacher's role in terms of giving back to the fraternity and the community at large (Lee & Low, 2014b). For example, an early emphasis on collaborative learning and group projects in preservice programs in NIE helps to sow the seeds for professional learning and sharing when preservice teachers become beginning teachers. The mentorship that student teachers receive in practicum is another experience that can help deepen their commitment to contributing to the community and teaching fraternity (Lee & Low, 2014b). Apart from courses and practica that help strengthen professional values among preservice teachers, NIE's introduction of core mandatory programs focusing on values development—such as Meranti, a personal and professional development workshop, and Group Endeavours in Service Learning (GESL) program, a mandatory community development project—enact the belief that values can not only "be taught through the formal curriculum," but also can "be caught through experiential learning platforms such as service learning" (Lee & Low, 2014b, p. 61). The two programs are described in detail later in the section entitled "Values Development."

Alongside the V^{3}SK framework is the articulation of the Graduand Teacher Competencies (GTCs), which outline the professional standards, benchmarks, and goals for graduands of NIE's ITP programs (see Table 3.) These competencies are modeled after MOE's teacher appraisal and development system—the Enhanced Performance Management System (EPMS)—and specify three dimensions of preservice teachers' professional performance: professional practice, leadership and management, and personal effectiveness.

Table 3. GTC Framework from NIE.

Performance Dimensions	Core Competencies
Professional Practice	1. Nurturing the whole child 2. Providing quality learning of child 3. Providing quality learning of child in CCA 4. Cultivating knowledge: i. with subject mastery ii. with reflective thinking iii. with analytic thinking iv. with initiative v. with creative teaching vi. with a future focus

Performance Dimensions	Core Competencies
Leadership and Management	5. Winning hearts and minds i. Understanding the environment ii. Developing others 6. Working with others i. Partnering parents ii. Working in teams
Personal Effectiveness	7. Knowing self and others i. Tuning into self ii. Exercising personal integrity and legal responsibilities iii. Understanding and respecting others iv. Resilience and adaptability

Source: NIE, 2009, p. 53.

One can see that there is not a one-to-one correspondence between any individual value, skill, or type of knowledge articulated in the V³SK model with any of the GTCs. However, the influence of individual values, skills, and knowledge lies in the definition of each of the GTCs (NIE, 2009). GTCs suggest that beginning teachers who graduate from NIE's teacher preparation programs will have been adequately prepared to perform the core roles of nurturing the child and facilitating quality learning for their students. They will demonstrate strong subject content mastery and pedagogical content knowledge of the subjects they will teach. They will be able to work and respect others and will have developed values pertaining to self.

The changes in curriculum resulting from TE²¹ through V³SK and GTCs (see Lee & Low, 2014b for a complete summary) have also activated parallel changes in pedagogies and assessment. Key pedagogical changes include the transferring of learning from teachers to the students in order to develop self-directed and lifelong learners. For example, real-world learning encourages problem-based learning (PBL) where in the educational psychology courses, real-life, school-based scenarios are used as discussion focal points. Learners act as active problem-solvers while teachers act as mediating coaches. Another example is the student-led lessons implemented in a core educational studies course—social context of education. Pedagogy in teacher preparation is also enhanced by the enabling power of technology, as exemplified by the development and use of innovative software to enhance pedagogical development and the institute-wide sharing of the latest development of technological tools that can enrich teaching and learning.

In terms of assessment, the Assessment Competency Framework for 21st Century Teaching and Learning spells out a set of assessment literacy outcomes to be acquired and developed by teachers from the preservice through to the professional teaching stage. Key processes that enable both NIE educators and teachers to adopt innovative assessment practices *as*, *of*, and *for* learning were identified and scaled up across programs (e.g., peer critique of lesson plans). NIE faculty then mapped out the current assessment literacies covered in all the preservice courses according to the framework adapted from Boud and Falchikov (2007):

- Designing appropriate assessment tasks
- Planning assessment as part of effective teaching and learning
- Understanding and communicating goals
- Developing the capacity for self-assessment in order to build reflective and self-directed learners
- Providing feedback to help learners improve
- Administering, scoring, and interpreting effectively
- Recognizing objective and ethical procedures

(as cited in NIE, 2009, p. 96)

Different course coordinators constantly communicate with each other in order to ensure continuity and alignment in the range of assessment competencies covered in different courses. An online platform has been established to hold key readings on assessment *of* and *for* learning. In addition, preservice teachers are exposed to assessment literacies both at a broad level and at more subject/discipline-specific levels. The philosophy of assessment *for* and *of* learning is embraced in all efforts on assessment literacy in NIE (Lee & Low, 2014b). Throughout the program, structured reflection is encouraged and facilitated. In tandem with pedagogical innovations, the physical infrastructure for teaching and learning was reconfigured to facilitate collaborative and interactive learning in groups.

A third key initiative arising from TE^{21} recommendations is the fostering of tighter theory-practice linkages. This is done through a few ways. For example, in order to ensure that student teachers develop the metacognition needed to put the program components together into a coherent whole, they are required to maintain a teaching and learning electronic portfolio (e-portfolio). The e-portfolio is "an electronic collection of authentic and diverse evidence of a student teacher's learning and achievement over time, on which he/she has reflected and designed for personal development, as well as for presentation to audiences for specific purposes" (Chye et al., 2012, p. 55). It serves to document student teachers' growth and development of their personal teaching philosophies, capacities, and competencies over the course of their preservice preparation. It is called the Teaching and Learning Portfolio to emphasize its role in charting the development of a student teacher from preservice through to entry into the profession as a beginning teacher.

The main components of the ITP program (Link 11) may be divided into the following broad categories as shown in Table 4.

Below are brief explanations of each of the program components (refer to the NIE website for more detailed information on the programs, courses and syllabi: http://www.nie.edu.sg/office-teacher-education/programmes-courses).

Academic Subjects

Academic Subjects cover knowledge of the content and fundamental concepts and principles of either one or two subjects, depending on the program in which the student teacher is enrolled. For example, in the

Table 4. Main Components of the Preservice Teacher Preparation Programs.

Program Components	Areas of Focus
Academic subjects Subject knowledge	Content knowledge (academic and pedagogical)
Education studies	Educational philosophy, psychology, professional practice and inquiry, assessment, information and communication technology, etc.
Curriculum studies	Teaching methodology (discipline-specific)
Character and citizenship education Group endeavours in service learning Meranti project	Character and values development
Language enhancement and academic discourse skills	Oral and written communication
Practicum (teaching practice)	Field experience
Research component	Academic research project Educational inquiry project

case of a BA (Ed) (primary) student, the choice of the first academic subject must be an arts (i.e., humanities) subject (e.g., geography) while in the case of a BSc (Ed) (primary) student teacher, the academic subject must be a science subject (e.g., chemistry).

Different from the 16-month PGDE program, all student teachers enrolled in the four-year BA/BSc (Ed) program have the opportunity to pursue academic subjects (i.e., disciplinary content knowledge) in one field (for the primary track) and two fields, a major and minor (for secondary track candidates). The reason for this inclusion is candidates in the four-year program are pursuing their first degree and they therefore need to specialize in specific disciplines to earn their respective bachelor degrees: an arts discipline for the BA (Ed) or a science discipline for a BSc (Ed) degree. Thus, the four-year program integrates academic content with pedagogical methodology in a single degree. By contrast, candidates in the PGDE program have at least obtained a degree at the bachelor's level in a certain discipline. Therefore, in the 16-month PGDE program, candidates are not required to study academic subjects. However, candidates in the two-year PGDE (physical education) are required to read one academic subject—physical education.

Subject Knowledge

The group of courses under subject knowledge aims to help reinforce subject content mastery for primary school teaching. Primary track student teachers in the Dip Ed, BA/BSc (Ed), PGDE (primary) (art), and PGDE (primary) (general) programs must take subject knowledge subjects aligned with their choice of curriculum subjects.

Education Studies

The suite of courses under the umbrella of education studies covers many disciplines deemed essential for providing student teachers with the necessary foundation to understand their learners and ways to engage them. They equip student teachers with the key concepts and principles in education that are essential for effective instruction and reflective practice in schools. This includes educational psychology, professional inquiry and practice, classroom management, information and communication technology, and assessment literacy courses, focusing on core educational concepts such as pupil development, the learning and thinking process, the social context within which schooling operates, the application of psychology in teaching and learning, assessment literacy, and the use of instructional technologies. The aim is to provide a sound theoretical base which teachers can tap so as to reflect on their practice in the future. The courses are pivoted on NIE's values-based V^3SK framework and the GTCs framework, as well as MOE's 21CC framework.

Curriculum Studies

Curriculum studies aim to equip student teachers with pedagogical methodologies for teaching specific subjects. In the primary track, student teachers are prepared to teach two or three subjects. Most primary student teachers will take the general combination English language, mathematics, and science with a small group of student teachers taking two of the general combination subjects and social studies. For the BA/BSc (Ed) secondary track, student teachers take two subjects including a major (Academic Studies 1 and Curriculum Studies 1) and a minor (Academic Studies 2 and Curriculum Studies 2), with academic studies and curriculum studies matching each other (e.g., English [Academic Studies] + English [Curriculum Studies]). For the PGDE secondary track, student teachers also take two subjects with a major (Curriculum Studies 1) and minor (Curriculum Studies 2) combination. The entry criteria for the major subject and minor subject are different, with the major subject having more stringent standards. The rationale for the differentiation of two subjects is that teachers need depth of knowledge in the subjects that they are teaching. After they graduate, most of them teach two subjects. However, the expectation is that student teachers should be able to teach all levels in secondary school for their major but only at the lower secondary levels for their minor subject.

Values Development

Given the focus on values development in NIE's teacher education model, a range of initiatives have been introduced based on the philosophy that values can be both taught and caught. There are three mandatory programs in which student teachers participate: a course entitled Character and Citizenship Education (CCE); the Group Endeavours in Service Learning (GESL); and the Meranti Project. The overall objectives of these initiatives include:

> Helping student teachers to develop better self-awareness (better tuning into self); providing a clearer idea of what NE [National

> Education] and CCE is all about and one's role in nurturing NE and CCE in innovative ways in the classroom; better ideas of working with diversity in the classroom; strategies for coping with being a teacher; and an affirmation of choosing teaching as a career. (Lee & Low, 2014b, p. 61)

The new course on CCE was introduced in the preservice curriculum in 2014, in tandem with the ministry's introduction of this course in the school curriculum. It helps student teachers to understand the key concepts in CCE and get a good grasp of their roles and professional commitments to CCE in school. For example, student teachers will learn about character development, elements of citizenship, key approaches for CCE, and current MOE policy and curriculum related to CCE. In addition, they will acquire the relevant knowledge and skills needed to deliver CCE in school.

GESL is a mandatory community involvement project. It aims to help student teachers build strong partnerships with the community by requiring them to engage with communities of their choice in groups of 20, spend at least 20 hours of contact time with the selected community, and to produce a tangible end product. GESL aims to broaden student teachers' knowledge and understanding of underserved communities. Through a hands-on approach, it hopes to develop student teachers' social-emotional learning competencies, project management skills, teamwork, needs analysis, decision-making, and empathy toward diverse communities around them. Each group decides on the service and learning objectives before the commencement of the project. To facilitate the process, each group is assigned a staff mentor who mentors, guides, and eventually assesses the group's project. Student teachers assuming different roles in their GESL group (e.g., leader, facilitator, secretary) also receive targeted training in terms of their roles and relevant skills.

An example of a GESL project is one where students decided to work with the Retinitis Pigmentosa (RP) Society, whose members are sufferers of RP, a debilitating eye disease that affects approximately 10% of Singapore's population. The group raised S$5,500 that they used to purchase assistive technology which can enlarge print up to 60 times for RP sufferers, which the society now loans to those who need it. Next, the group, in close consultation with ophthalmologists, also produced a brochure about RP to promote public awareness about the condition.

The Meranti Project is another meaningful initiative within the area of character and values development. The Meranti Project gets its name from the Meranti tree which produces very hard wood, and the symbolism is that the project aims to produce resilient teachers. It is a two-day session facilitated by carefully selected external vendors who conduct sessions where student teachers reflect upon their life journeys and reasons for joining teaching and interact with in-service teachers and students in order to be able to understand the present day realities of teaching in school.

Language Enhancement and Academic Discourse Skills

NIE's teacher education programs also have an important component for developing student teachers' competencies for effective oral and written communication in the classroom, which is known as Language Enhancement and Academic Discourse Skills (LEADS). This comprises two main courses, one that builds oral communication skills via introduction to basic phonetics, voice projection, and oral presentation techniques, and another that focuses on the genre of written academic discourse required for fulfilling assignments, reports, and theses required at the undergraduate phase.

Research

Research is another component that features strongly in NIE's teacher education programs. For example, in year 3, TSP candidates are required to read a module entitled Research Project, which is an introductory course into research. It aims to "provide an unparalleled opportunity for student teachers and faculty members to explore a topic of mutual interest together, following a spontaneous flow of dialog and intellectual exchange in the spirit of learning" (NIE, 2015, p. 110). Student teachers who are non-TSP candidates also take part in an introductory course in research, in which they work with a faculty mentor to complete a research project on an educational topic. The course aims to "help student teachers gain an understanding of the scientific methods behind research; learn methods of designing, collecting, analyzing and interpreting data using examples from a variety of specialty areas in education; conduct a research project that helps student teachers to think more critically about research in general" (NIE, 2015, p. 109).

A key component of the preservice teacher education programs is the practicum or clinical field experience. The clinical field experience is a crucial lynchpin to link theory to practice, especially in a university-based model of teacher education such as the one offered in Singapore.

For that reason, it deserves its own section especially given the enhanced practicum model introduced since 2009.

Practicum and Field Experience[5]

Practicum has always been regarded as an essential component of strong teacher education programs (Darling-Hammond & Hammerness, 2005; Tan & Liu, 2014; Hairon, Goh, & Teng, 2014). Over the past decade, NIE's framework for practicum has undergone several refinements in tandem with NIE's aspiration to stay relevant and responsive to the fast-changing educational landscape and the overall enhancement of teacher preparation programs (Hairon et al., 2014). This section describes the recent improvements in preservice teachers' field experiences, which can be encapsulated by the commonly known Enhanced Practicum Model. Before we delve into the detailed features of improvement, it is important to introduce the general structure of practicum in the major initial teacher preparation programs in NIE.

The practicum structure for the four-year undergraduate and the 16-month postgraduate program is shown in Table 5.

The practicum component comprises about 20% of the total program component (or 22 weeks) of the four-year undergraduate program while it takes up about 35% (or 14 weeks) of the 16-month postgraduate program. The practicum postings are designed to be developmental in nature where each posting is structured to build student teachers' teaching competencies in developmental, incremental phases (NIE, n.d.g.). Their school experiences serve as a critical resource for student teachers' discussions and reflections in coursework at NIE and are helpful in deepening their understanding of both theory and practice. The school experience for BA/BSc (Ed) students takes place at the end of the candidate's first year of preservice education and placement is for one week

Table 5. Practicum Structure for the BA/BSc (Ed) and the 16-Month PGDE.

Type (Duration)	BA/BSc (Ed)	PGDE
School experience	2 weeks	N.A.
Teaching assistantship	5 weeks	4 weeks
Teaching practice 1	5 weeks	N.A.
Teaching practice 2	10 weeks	10 weeks

in a primary school, with a second week in a secondary school. There are only observations required in this first posting because the purpose is to expose student teachers to the realities of the classroom and school setting. The student teachers are required to collect observation data, which are used for their coursework when they return to NIE. The teaching assistantship (TA) comprising five weeks for the BA/BSc programs and four weeks for the PGDE program enables student teachers to observe and reflect on lessons conducted by their cooperating teachers (CTs) and other experienced teachers. Through assisted teaching, they gain hands-on experience by helping their CTs plan parts of the lessons, prepare classroom resources, and manage students. During TA, BA/BSC (Ed) student teachers write and submit weekly reflections to their NIE faculty supervisor. PGDE student teachers' TA is organized in a way that they spend four days in school and one day in NIE each week. At NIE, they meet their tutors for curriculum studies and their tutor for pedagogical practices. The aim of the teaching assistantship is to strengthen the theory-practice link and provide students with an opportunity to develop an understanding of their future role as a teacher and experience firsthand the challenges of teaching in the local context. Teaching Practice 1 lasts for five weeks; student teachers still have opportunities initially to observe CTs' lessons but also plan their own lessons and resources and begin to teach independently, applying what they have learned in NIE, while still being guided by their CTs and NIE faculty supervisor.

The final practicum posting (Teaching Practice 2) is, in many contexts, the main practicum posting (the rest have been called pre-practicum postings in other contexts such as the United States), and this runs for 10 weeks for both the 4-year and the 16-month programs. The main aim of this final practicum is to allow student teachers to acquire the range of teaching competencies required of a beginning teacher, including planning, developing resources and teaching lessons, managing the classroom effectively, and being exposed to the wider roles and responsibilities that teachers assume when they graduate from preservice. These include conducting cocurricular activities and participating in other auxiliary roles such as attending meetings and being involved in school events. Student teachers are expected to teach entire lessons on their own and are observed informally (not graded) and then formally (with grades awarded).

NIE's enhanced practicum model is framed by the view of preparing teachers to be thinkers and professionals (Liu, Tan, & Hairon, 2014), rather than developing them into "technician, consumer, receiver, transmitter, and implementer of other people's knowledge" (Cochran-Smith & Lytle, 1999, p. 16). According to Tan, Liu, and Low (2012), the preparation of thinking teachers emphasizes thinking in context and encompasses three elements: skillful teaching, reflective teaching, and innovative teaching. Specifically, NIE's aspiration is to develop teachers who are reflective about their professional roles, think systematically about their practices, make effective use of theories and research, are adaptive and innovative in teaching to better support students' learning, and take the initiative and responsibility for their own learning and professional development (Tan & Liu, 2014). The enhanced practicum model is one of NIE's key endeavors to meet the challenge of developing teachers who can "learn from teaching" and "learn for teaching" (Darling-Hammond, 2006).

The enhanced practicum model is based on three key foundations and five tenets (Liu et al., 2014, pp. 110–113). The first foundation is the philosophical stance of teaching as a professional thinking activity. Based on this philosophy, practicum aims to provide a platform for professional practice and reflection for preservice teachers. The second foundation is a strong NIE-school partnership that ensures all parties work toward the common endeavor of teacher preparation. The third foundation is the essence of strengthening theory-practice links. In NIE, the theory-practice nexus is strengthened through reflection, experiential learning, school-based research projects, the use of authentic classroom materials, and pedagogical tools on campus that simulate real classroom settings (Liu et al., 2014).

Other important factors that bridge the theory-practice gap include the cohesive design of the entire program, the use of e-portfolio, the introduction of planned and structured reflection, and the introduction of focused professional conversations (Tan & Liu, 2014). Planned and structured reflection invites student teachers to mentally restructure an experience or a problem and actively reflect on their practices to see where and how they can improve (*SingTeach*, 2010). Student teachers are required to attend three focused professional conversations facilitated by the school coordinating mentors or other senior teachers in their practicum schools. The first takes place at the beginning of practicum and asks student teachers to share their learning experiences at NIE and what they have learned about teaching and learning. The second conversation falls in the middle of practicum and invites student teachers to bring up issues that they are facing for discussion, such as classroom management, motivating students, and instructional strategies. The last conversation takes place at the end of practicum. Student teachers share how practicum has helped them develop as teachers, with reference to GTCs. (Please refer to the practicum handbook for more details about these programs: http://www.nie.edu.sg/files/practicum/Handbook/Practicum_Handbook_2015.pdf.)

In addition to the three foundations, NIE's enhanced practicum model is designed around five key tenets (Liu et al., 2014): (1) making practicum an integrated part of a coherent program to have greater impact on preservice teachers' conceptions and practices; (2) providing instructional and psychological support through purposeful mentoring from experienced teachers and university supervisors; (3) allowing preservice teachers to develop their professional competency through graduated responsibility and opportunities for practice; (4) assessing preservice teachers holistically through both formative and summative measures with clearly defined standards that go beyond pedagogical content knowledge; (5) making use of planned and structured reflection, and focused professional conversations for the purpose of developing thinking teachers.

The foundations and tenets of the enhanced practicum model are essential in developing the *autonomous thinking* teachers for the 21st century that NIE envisions (Liu et al., 2014; Tan & Liu, 2014). The purpose is to empower student teachers with both a sound knowledge base to inform their practice, as well as practice that can deepen their understanding of theoretical concepts (Darling-Hammond, 2006; Tan & Liu, 2014). In addition, the teacher education programs also aim to develop student teachers' positive attitudes toward teaching as well as a strong commitment to their students and their profession (Tan & Liu, 2014).

This section has covered much of the third theme of a high-quality teaching workforce in two main parts, recruiting, and preparing high-quality teachers. As graduates formally enter the profession, their transition from student teacher to teacher of students is supported by a variety of mentoring and induction supports, which move the story to the next stage of quality teaching and teachers—nurturing and retaining quality.

THEME 4: DEVELOPMENTAL AND EDUCATIVE APPRAISAL FOR ONGOING LEARNING

Nurturing and Retaining Quality: Beginning Teacher Induction

The importance and seriousness of ITP in Singapore is signaled by the Teachers' Pledge, first at the start of candidates' program at a ceremony known as the Teachers' Compass Ceremony (TCC) and then at the graduation ceremony known as the Teachers' Investiture Ceremony. The Teachers' Investiture Ceremony is attended by the minister of education, as well as faculty and administrators at NIE, including senior management, such as the director and deans, and is reported in the public media. The ceremony runs over the course of a week and represents an important initiation ritual for all new teachers to "strengthen their identity as to who teachers are and what they represent" (Lee & Low, 2014b, p. 57). In reciting this pledge as they enter the profession, novice teachers voice aloud their commitments and responsibilities as teachers:

> We, the teachers of Singapore, pledge that:
>
> - We will be true to our mission to bring out the best in our students.
> - We will be exemplary in the discharge of our duties and responsibilities.
> - We will guide our students to be good and useful citizens of Singapore.
> - We will continue to learn and pass on the love of learning to our students.
> - We will win the trust, support, and co-operation of parents and the community so as to enable us to achieve our mission. (MOE, n.d.a.)

The pledge has been articulated in the Ethos of the Teaching Profession (AST, n.d.b.) and underscores a national vision of teachers as valuable professionals. Teachers' professional development is conceived as a continuous journey with ITP as only the first stage of this process.

Therefore, it is acknowledged that "no preservice teacher preparation programs can fully prepare teachers with all the competencies of a professional teacher" within a finite period of time (Lee & Low, 2014b, p. 56). It is assumed that competencies can be further developed during the span of a teacher's career through professional learning (Lee & Low, 2014b).

Upon graduating from their preservice programs, all beginning teachers (BTs) are provided—according to their content specialization and the needs of schools—with induction support that is centrally managed by MOE. Induction spans novice teachers' first two years of teaching. Virtually all new teachers (99%) are immersed in formal induction programs, a level much higher than the average of the countries that participated in the Teaching and Learning International Survey (TALIS) (OECD, 2014b). A comprehensive teacher induction program known as the Beginning Teachers' Induction Program (BTIP) is provided by AST to "establish even and high standards of professional expertise across the fraternity" (AST, n.d.a.). Funding for all BTIP programs comes from MOE, which has as a primary objective to help BTs experience success and to enhance their passion, conviction, and beliefs in/of teaching. This two-year induction program helps BTs transition from preservice to in-service professional learning and strives to provide BTs with:

- an understanding of their roles and responsibilities, as well as the professional expectations and ethos of the teaching service;
- the opportunity to take ownership of their professional growth and development;
- a sense of belonging to the teaching fraternity; and
- a support structure for their personal well-being (AST, n.d.a.)

Portrait of Practice

There is a clear and comprehensive induction system at RGS, which involves various personnel in the school, including buddies, senior teachers, HOD for professional development, program owners (coordinators), research experts at PeRL, and the senior management. Each party has a clear role and responsibility in terms of supporting the professional learning of BTs. The induction program mentioned in this portrait is meant for not only BTs but all teachers new to RGS.

> The program not only involves general introductions of the school, but also a clear emphasis on continuous learning of the teacher to prepare them for the needs of the talented students at the school.
>
> We have a system and structure that specifically looks at the development of BTs. There is a one-day induction by the principal, vice principals, and all the program owners. In the subsequent one year, there will be modules for BTs conducted by different personnel, covering a whole range of their work as an RGS teacher. The modules cover a wide range of areas such as how to teach critical thinking, and how to facilitate the social emotional learning of the gifted girls. After the teacher is inducted to RGS, there is a total learning plan for all staff every year.
>
> Mrs. Poh Mun See, Principal, Raffles Girls' School

Figure 6 lays out the structure of the teacher induction framework. While it starts, in essence with the Teachers' Compass Ceremony before the start of preservice preparation, it picks up post graduation with the Beginning Teachers' Orientation Program (BTOP). Within the first two years, BTs attend in-service courses designed specifically for them, are exposed to school-based mentoring, and visit the MOE Heritage Centre. The two-year journey concludes with the Beginning Teachers' Symposium. Once BTs enter into the third year of their professional life, they are considered to be experienced teachers. What follows is a brief description of the various stages and components in the framework.

Figure 6. MOE Teacher Induction Framework.

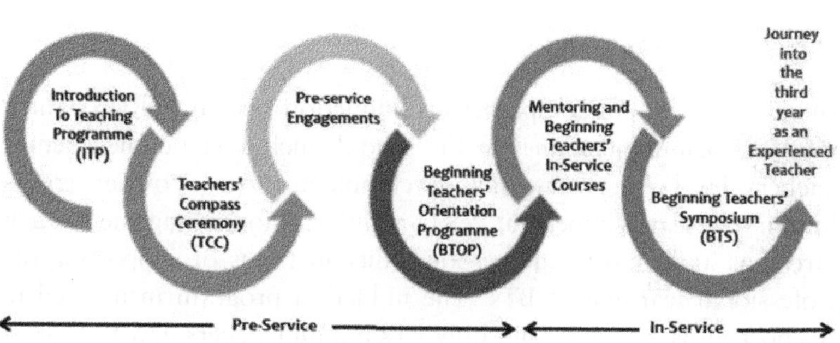

Source: AST, n.d.a.

Beginning Teachers' Orientation Program (BTOP)

Post graduation, BTs participate in a three-day BTOP, which allows them to consolidate their learning; understand their roles and the expectations of the profession; reflect on their personal beliefs, values, and practices within the context of the larger fraternity; and recognize the importance of nurturing the whole child (AST, n.d.a.). These expectations, roles, beliefs, and values are articulated in the Ethos of the Teaching Profession to guide the conduct of teachers and ensure that they meet the standards of the profession.

In-service Courses (for BTs)

Building on the foundations laid by NIE, the in-service courses serve to further enhance BTs' professional competencies. The courses cover a wide range of topics, such as classroom management, parent engagement, teacher-student relationships, reflective practice, pedagogies, and assessment literacy. In addition, BTs are encouraged to complete an online course for newly appointed civil servants: Public Service Orientation Kit (AST, n.d.a.).

MOE Heritage Centre (HC) Visit

The MOE HC was recently constructed as a place to "showcase Singapore's Education Story from the early 19th century to the present," to affirm the work of currently serving educators, and to celebrate the contributions of pioneer educators and communities that have shaped the education system in Singapore (MOE HC, n.d.). The gallery exhibits highlight every phase of the nation's development and the role education played (Heng, 2011). In addition, the center contains interactive and reflective galleries for visitors to reflect and reminisce on their past experiences as students (Heng, 2011). The aim of the MOE HC visit is to "deepen BTs' understanding and appreciation of the role of education in nation building" (AST, n.d.a.). In addition, it aims to foster BTs' "sense of pride and belonging to the teaching fraternity" (AST, n.d.a.).

Beginning Teachers' (BT) Symposium

The symposium serves as a platform to promote teacher ownership and teacher leadership among BTs. Its stated theme is: "What Matters Most: Purpose, Passion, and Professionalism," which calls for effective practices and strong commitment to the profession. This symposium happens at the end of BTs' second year; thereafter they are no longer considered as BTs but experienced teachers.

Collectively, these BTIP programs help BTs to bridge the gap between their preservice and in-service learning. They serve as the initial level courses of professional development, which can be extended to higher levels during further professional learning.

Structured Mentoring Program (SMP)

Besides the induction program in place for BTs, the schools they enter typically have in place a systemic framework for school-based mentoring. Mentoring arrangements and programs are typically overseen by the school staff developer (SSD) and teacher leaders. One of the many school-based mentoring programs is known as the Structured Mentoring Program (SMP), launched on January 27, 2006. The aim of SMP is to level up the standard of induction and mentoring practices, which historically varied across schools, and enable BTs to gain knowledge within a community of practice with the support of a more experienced peer. In leveling up the standard of induction and mentoring practices, SMP has defined mentoring and induction as a schoolwide practice that benefits all teachers and encourages growth. Thus, as one interviewee stated, "Even the principal, vice principal, see me, they will check with me how I am getting on, give me advice" because the goal of mentoring support is ultimately, "if I teach you right, you'll get better (as a teacher)."

The SMP conceptual framework (Figure 7) consists of three main dimensions: induction, school-level mentoring, and the BT Learning Program.

School-level mentoring is seen as crucial to BTs. The guidance and coaching BTs receive from experienced mentors help them effectively transfer and translate their learning in preservice preparation into their classrooms and learn practical knowledge and skills in teaching (AST, n.d.a.). Regular conversations are held between teachers and their mentors, who are usually senior and lead teachers in schools.

There is therefore a need for mentors to understand the main goals of mentoring, which are induction to the school community; BTs' professional development; and BTs' growth in terms of helping them realize their personal and professional aspirations. TALIS results indicate that among all countries in the study, Singapore has the highest ratio of teachers serving as mentors (39%) or who currently have an assigned

Figure 7. Key Components of the Structured Mentoring Program for BTs.

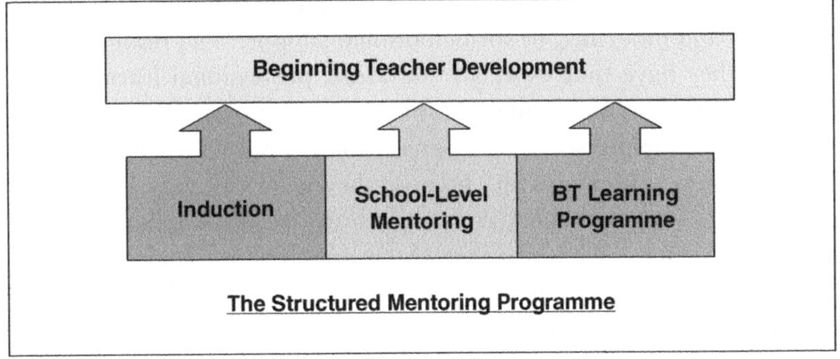

Source: Chong & Tan, 2006, p. 5.

mentor (40%), in sharp contrast to the TALIS averages of 14% and 13%, respectively (OECD, 2014b). In addition, of particular importance is the fact that 85% of the mentees are assigned to mentors who teach the same subject, compared to the TALIS average of 68% (OECD, 2014b).

To ensure better training and clearer expectations of mentors, the MOE created a Skillful Teaching and Enhanced Mentoring (STEM) (Link 12) program in 2011. The aims of STEM include discovering good models and practices for the mentoring of BTs and ensuring more even mentoring practices, thereby leveling up the quality of teaching across schools. This initiative began with 30 prototype schools and included the training of in-service teachers. In 2016, there are now 120 STEM schools. Under STEM, the Mentor Preparation Programme (MPP) was developed with the New Teacher Centre (USA). It focused on the professional development (PD) of instructional mentors, which intensively prepared them with the mentoring language, tools, and processes to deepen their practice in supporting BTs' learning.

Mentors serve in different capacities. There is usually a mentor coordinator who leads and drives the school's mentoring program and acts as the "mentor for mentors" so that the mentoring goals at the school level can be achieved (Janas, 1996). Then there is the mentor, usually a more experienced teacher or teacher leader (e.g., senior teacher, lead teacher) who serves as a pillar of professional support for BTs as they continue to hone their professional competencies. The mentors would typically have received PD to prepare them for this mentoring role as it is a central part of their job.

Mentoring is a compulsory part of being a teacher leader (i.e., senior, lead, and master teachers). Teacher leaders are typically given primary responsibility for supporting and mentoring new teachers, support that runs the gamut from technical assistance, subject-specific pedagogical leadership and modeling, to socioemotional support: PD; resource sharing, etc. They have time especially set aside, professional learning provided, and expectations formalized for mentoring novices. New teachers we interviewed expressed their appreciation of "all the mentors I had, all the teachers I worked with" because they were "all very supportive, quite caring. They will check constantly how are you coping, any help they need to offer." We heard that "Mentors try to use [mentee's] prior knowledge. . .[to]. . . try and build on [mentee's] strengths" and help new teachers come to "know about school culture, what are the expectations, some of the 'dos' and 'don'ts.'" In interviews, respondents felt that help was constantly available to them, "I don't even need to ask 'Can I borrow?' [Mentors] will say, 'Come and take.' So I think it's a very good environment. . . everyone is helpful."

We also learned that mentors support their mentees in going beyond the immediacy of daily practice, by encouraging them to build their knowledge. Mentors "will ask you things like, 'Have you heard of this concept called, say, tacit learning? No, right? It's quite new you know. Maybe you should know about it. I don't really agree with it. Let me know what you think. '" Or maybe one might "sit down next to you and say, 'I'm reading this book. It's really interesting. Why don't you read a few pages and tell me what you think about it?'"

Ms. Tan Hwee Pin, principal of Kranji Secondary School, described the support for beginning teachers in this way:

> We welcome our BTs to our school as part of our Kranji family. It is important to induct them into our school's culture so that they know the role that they play and the expectations and standards required when they interact with our students. Our mentoring programme is led by a team of seven senior teachers, under the advice of our vice-principal. Every BT or trainee will be given an experienced teacher as their mentor. BTs not only observe lessons of their subject areas, but also teachers from other subjects; I believe that every subject teacher has different strengths and they employ different pedagogies in different disciplines. By casting the net wider, new teachers will be able to assemble a repertoire of strategies, which they can activate when they become a full-fledged teacher.

Senior teacher, Mdm. Rosmiliah Bte Kasmin elaborates:

> BTs are attached to a particular senior teacher. On the first day of school, the senior teachers welcome BTs in the morning, introduce them to the school, and go through the induction program with them. The program will include topics such as timetabling, how to take leave, how to carry themselves as a professional in school, and also make sure they have a proper workstation. They also bring BTs to meet with the senior management for an introduction and chat, just to make sure that they feel welcomed in the school.

Besides the help that BTs get from senior teachers, schools also have a buddy system. The buddy is usually someone who is teaching the same subject as the BT, since the senior teacher may or may not be teaching the same subject. The mentor's responsibility is more of grooming the new teacher in terms of the pedagogical dimension, while the buddy usually serves as a more immediate contact when the BT needs help in administrative matters, a source of information on the department or school, as well as a friendly face and a listener. Talking about how the mentoring program helped him professionally when he was a new teacher, Mr. Azahar Bin Mohamed Noor (RGS), shared:

> To me what really helps as a new teacher is the mentoring and a buddy system. That is the most important. Knowing that you can actually approach somebody at any time of the day, and that person is very open to listening to you, it helps a lot.

BTs are typically given about 80% of the teaching workload of an experienced teacher, during which they are also subject to confirmation. The reduced workload is to provide the additional time and space for BTs to grow into their profession. In Singapore, the probationary period for BTs is one year. Once teachers are confirmed, they do not need to be recertified or licensed. Thus, confirmation has been taken to be analogous to having tenure. Sclafani and Lim (2008) observe:

> New teachers are observed and coached by grade-level chairs, subject area chairs, and heads of departments. If a teacher is not performing well, additional support and coaching come into play. Everyone tries to help the new teacher adjust and improve, but lack of improvement, poor attitude or lack of professionalism is not tolerated. . .[T]he new teacher may be allowed to try another school, but if a year of working with the teacher has not improved his or her performance, the teacher may be asked to leave the profession. The system believes

> that it should do its best up front and counsel out those who do not make progress despite the support and assistance. Past this milestone, very few teachers are asked to leave, and then the causes may be lack of integrity, inappropriate behavior with a student, financial mismanagement, or racial insensitivity. (p. 4)

Note that the one-year probation period should not be confused with the two-year induction for all BTs. In other words, the confirmation after probation is not tied to the completion of the two-year induction period.

Professional Learning and Recognition

Retaining quality within the profession is not just about ensuring that BTs are carefully inducted into the profession, but also about ensuring that attrition rates remain low even after teachers have spent many years in the profession. In order to ensure that talent is retained within the profession, the ministry announced the GROW package in 2006, which was designed for the professional and personal Growth of education officers, through better Recognition, Opportunities, and seeing to their Well-being (MOE, 2007). The package created more opportunities for teachers to develop and strengthen their core competencies, provided more career options and choices, and gave greater recognition to the everyday work of teachers.

Since then, there has been an updated GROW 2.0 package, and the summary of the enhancements are shown in Table 6.

Table 6. Summary of GROW 2.0 Initiatives

Well-being • Expansion of part-time teaching scheme • Greater support for part-time teaching • Enhancements to no-pay leave	Growth • Professional development packages • Greater support for postgraduate studies • More in-service upgrading opportunities for non-graduate teachers
Opportunities • Enhanced senior specialist track • Further reemployment opportunities • Future leaders program	Recognition • New education scheme of service (2008) • Revised incentive plan • Additional outstanding contribution awards

Source: MOE, 2007.

The main initiatives in GROW 2.0 are described in detail in the May 2008 issue of MOE's *Contact: The Teachers' Digest* (http://www.moe.gov.sg/corporate/contactprint/pdf/contact_may08.pdf) and MOE's press release entitled "Putting People at the Centre of the Education Enterprise" on 28 December, 2007 (http://www.moe.gov.sg/media/press/2007/pr20071228.htm), but will be briefly summarized here according to the order of growth, opportunities, recognition, and well-being. The first is growth. In line with MOE's emphasis on lifelong learning and continuing education, GROW 2.0 provides a range of PD packages to help graduate and nongraduate teachers improve themselves academically. There is greater support for postgraduate studies in terms of offering full-pay study leave for teachers who want to pursue master's/doctoral studies and more teacher posts for schools that have teachers pursuing full-time postgraduate studies. Nongraduate teachers can attend part-time on-campus degrees offered by local universities, including NIE and Singapore Institute of Management University. In 2014, Mr. Heng Swee Keat, the Minister for Education, announced a new performance-based emplacement (promotion to a new position and salary scale) framework that enhances the career progression of nongraduate teachers. Nongraduate teachers, who have demonstrated outstanding performance, will be placed on the graduate salary scale without the need to obtain a degree. Previously, an experienced nongraduate teacher was not able to cross over to the graduate salary scale without a degree despite his or her outstanding contributions (Heng, 2014).

The second is recognition. To reward and retain outstanding teachers, MOE implemented a new Education Scheme of Service in April 2008, which set new salary ranges, variable merit increments, higher performance bonuses, additional annual bonuses, and a one-off salary increment. Teachers can also expect greater recognition in the form of additional outstanding contribution awards (OCAs). MOE also enhanced the CONNECT Plan (CONtiNuity, Experience, and Commitment in Teaching), which is a long-term incentive plan for teachers that gives teachers bonus payouts throughout their career. The new plan provides teachers with higher total career deposits, higher payouts in the first 20 years of a teacher's career when he or she may have higher financial commitments such as raising a family, and more flexibility in terms of when teachers can draw out their CONNECT balances.

The third is opportunities. The senior specialist track (SST) has been enhanced to provide more SST posts and improved career advancement and development opportunities. MOE also provided further reemployment opportunities for education officers beyond the age of 62—those who have good performance and are physically fit to work are offered reemployment as contract adjunct teachers up to age 65. MOE has also developed a reemployment framework. Subject to availability and individual needs of the schools, school middle managers and officers at equivalent positions in MOE headquarters can also continue in their existing jobs. School leaders and senior officers may also be offered work on a project or contract basis. To help education officers with their retirement plans, MOE has put into place systemic measures such as providing a comprehensive list of jobs and assignments for officers to consider, career advancement plans, and retirement planning seminars. In addition, the Future Leaders Programme aims to develop, recognize, and retain teachers with the potential to assume key leadership roles through giving them challenging assignments and projects.

The fourth is well-being. The Part-Time Teaching Scheme (PTTS)—originally designed to allow more work flexibility for female teachers with children under the age of 6 and teachers aged 55 years or above—has been extended to both female and male teachers with children under 21 years of age. To support schools with teachers on full-time post-graduate studies, up to five more part-time teaching posts have been provided to each school cluster over and above the existing manpower grants for PTTS.

In addition, the enhancement to no-pay leave allows teachers to take time out to look after a young child or follow a spouse on an overseas work attachment. Previously, no-pay leave was only granted to female teachers for child care up to the child's third birthday. Now this scheme has been extended to both female and male teachers to take care of their children up to the fourth birthday. Teachers can now also apply to accompany their spouse for up to four years, instead of three years in the former scheme. Teachers who are returning to work after two or more years of no-pay leave are also provided with a refresher course to ensure smooth transition back to teaching.

Having described extensively the issue of maintaining, nurturing, and retaining quality within the profession at the institutional and systemic level, we now delve into educative and developmental appraisal at the individual level.

Maintaining and Retaining Quality

The ministry utilizes the Enhanced Performance Management System (EPMS) as a structured method of appraisal that is holistic in nature and customized to the role each teacher plays on the career path she or he has selected. These are the teaching, leadership, and specialist tracks which are an important component of teacher development and advancement and are described in fuller detail in the section entitled "Professional Development along Differentiated Career Tracks." The customizable nature of EPMS helps reporting officers (ROs), i.e., the staff's supervisor, to determine professional development needs, promotion prospects, and annual performance grades. The appraisal parameters in EPMS are multidimensional and support three main goals: self-evaluation; coaching and mentoring; and performance-linked recognition.

Essentially, EPMS lays out a range of professional competencies as the basis for teacher appraisal and development, which specifies teachers' performance in key result areas (KRAs). KRAs are categorized into three clusters: (1) student outcomes (quality learning of students, character development of students); (2) professional outcomes (professional development of self, professional development of others); and (3) organizational outcomes (contributions to projects/committee work). The KRAs are open-ended with no rating scale, which teachers will go through with their direct supervisors. EPMS also provides competency-based behavioral indicators to provide greater clarity on the competencies that could be observed while achieving KRAs effectively. Competency is divided into individual attributes (e.g., professional values and ethics), professional mastery (e.g., student-centric, values-driven practice), organizational excellence (e.g., visioning and planning), and effective collaboration (e.g., interpersonal relationships and skills). Evaluation results based on the EPMS system help determine teachers' choice of career track, needs for professional development, suitability for promotion, grade of performance, and bonus compensation.

As an appraisal and development tool, EPMS functions as both a formative and summative review of teachers' work. First, it is adopted as a self-evaluation tool for teachers. For example, it can help teachers identify areas of strength, assess their own ability to nurture the whole child, track their students' results, review teaching competencies, develop personal training and development plans, and articulate innovations and other contributions to school development. Second, EPMS forms a basis for coaching and mentoring. The work review cycle begins with one-on-one target setting at the start of the year conducted with the teacher's immediate supervisor, followed by a mid-year review and end-of-year appraisal. The review cycle helps specify areas for improvement and enables developmental and career pathways to be mapped.

EPMS serves as a basis for performance-linked recognition in terms of retaining and growing the pool of quality teachers, encouraging innovative teaching methods, providing timely promotions for teachers with the potential for higher-level responsibilities. Performance is linked to compensation through monetary (e.g., salary adjustments) and nonmonetary means (e.g., awards such as the Outstanding Youth in Education Award [OYEA], the Caring Teacher Award [CTA], and the President's Award for Teachers [PAT]) in order to recognize exemplary teachers in the profession. MOE also disburses grants in the form of outstanding contribution awards to deserving teachers, which could be at the individual or team level.[6] Schools do not need a mechanism for preventing an explosion in salary or performance bonuses, as these are carefully managed by MOE, who directly pays all teachers. Figure 8 illustrates performance-based monetary compensation according to the McKinsey Report (2009).

The summative appraisal at the end of the year also discusses the teacher's future potential, known as the current estimated potential (CEP). The decision on potential is made based on evidence in the teacher's portfolio plus the supervisor's judgment of the teacher's contributions to the school and community, in consultation with the senior teachers who have worked with the teacher, the department chairs, the reporting officer, the vice principal, and the principal. CEP is used to help school leaders groom potential future leaders for the system and to ensure that they are given maximal exposure to PD activities that are geared toward helping these teachers to realize their CEP.

The evidence that we have collected from schools suggests that appraisal in Singapore schools is done in an educative and developmental way. The conversation between teachers and their ROs not only covers what they have done well and why, but also the gaps and areas where improvement may be needed. The Teacher Growth Model (TGM) with its comprehensive set of necessary competencies for teacher growth often guides these developmental conversations. The appraisal process is educative in a sense that after the conversation with the reporting officer, teachers compose their self-appraisal where they write down their thoughts and plans for the future, addressing questions such as: In what ways have you improved? How you are going to improve yourself further? What are the learning activities that you would like to take on? The evaluative aspect of EPMS emphasizes teaching and learning, contribution to committees and CCAs, and vital qualities of teachers such as professionalism

or integrity. The developmental aspect of EPMS (Link 13) is reflected in the sense that the conversation between the teacher and his/her reporting officer is ongoing throughout the year.

Figure 8. Singapore's Performance-Based Compensation.

Singapore has an established system of performance-based compensation

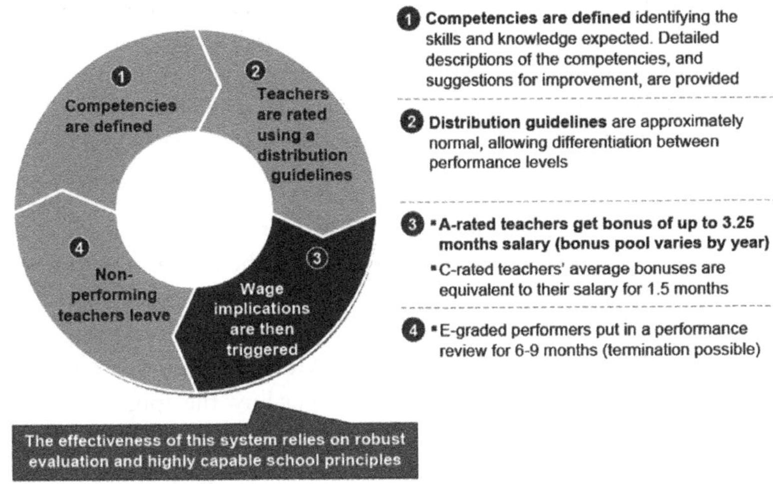

SOURCE: Team Analysis; NIE

Source: McKinsey and Co., 2009, p. 36.

Ms. Tan Hwee Pin, the principal of Kranji Secondary School, explained:

> We want to emphasise to the teachers that this is a developmental process. It is a journey and we want them to have ownership of this journey. Our HODs work with the teachers very closely and they provide feedback on a regular basis. This ongoing conversation enables teachers to chart their progress and develop their plans throughout the year.

Mr. Azahar Bin Mohamed Noor, a teacher-specialist at RGS, also emphasized the developmental nature of evaluation:

> Assessment is both evaluative and developmental. The conversation is done in a very developmental way. We have our own tools such as a classroom observation tool to assess teaching competency. We also use EPMS, where we have two conversations a year with our RO. The EPMS is to document what are our plans for the year, what we

> have done, and the impact it has on the school or the students. It also records teachers' training needs.
>
> For a struggling teacher, the conversation with the RO is very important. The conversation is ongoing, done at mid-year and end-of-year. During the conversations, he/she would have been told the areas that he/she needs to improve. So a struggling teacher would at least have some kind of intervention. The RO will set clear expectations for the teacher and see if he/she can meet them in the next half of the year. However, if a teacher is struggling, it could also be due to circumstance of family and other personal matters. These will be acknowledged in the conversations as well.

The evaluation also helps teachers clarify their career options. If any is thinking of taking up a particular career track, the appraisal and development processes will help inform the areas to which teachers need to pay special attention. As she herself converted from the leadership track to the teaching track (as a senior teacher), Mdm. Rosmiliah Bte Kasmin of Kranji Secondary School also shared with us how the appraisal helped her specifically to refocus on her professional development(Link 14):

> At the beginning of every year, you discuss with the Head your career options for the next 3 to 5 years, taking into consideration the teacher's performance in the previous year. That particular conversation will help you see which direction you would like to go. For example, if you intend to take up the leadership track as the Head of Department, for example, probably the school needs to expose you a bit more to different projects and responsibilities in the school. If you choose the teaching track, there are certain projects and things that you need to complete, or certain skills that you need to have before you can get to be promoted to the Senior Teacher position.
>
> When I was on the leadership track, I was doing more of activity organisation for the students at the departmental level and was not very involved in mentoring teachers directly. So with the appraisal, I could narrow down the kind of skills that I need to mentor the teachers and exactly how I can improve on my mentoring of the teachers. Rather than being the authority figure, I have to become more of a teacher mentor. There is a stark difference between a leadership position and a senior teacher position. A senior teacher is one whom teachers find approachable in talking to and comfortable getting advice from.

Independent schools do follow the MOE EPMS system. However, the system is adapted to suit the needs of the unique context of independent schools, where the expectations and roles of teachers are quite different from mainstream government schools. For example, in RGS, the lens that is adopted to appraise teachers is their ability to motivate the high-ability girls. Therefore, the appraisal places more emphasis on advanced content, higher-order thinking and processes, and conceptual learning. Its format is similar to MOE's, which includes performance planning at the beginning of the year, mid-year work review, and year-end work review. These procedures are essential steps in helping teachers understand where they are in terms of their own development and performance.

The appraisal system in independent schools is also generally divided among the different career tracks, namely, the teaching track, the leadership track, and the teacher specialist track, yet with small differences. For example, in RGS, the specialist track is different from that of the MOE. While MOE's specialist track is only for those who specialize in a specific area and do not teach in classrooms, the specialist track in RGS does include teachers. However, at RGS, teachers in the specialist track are partially released from teaching, and the freed-up time is used for educational research. Therefore, these teachers are specialists in education research. Still, many MOE specialists are teachers by training. Once they are on board the specialist track, some are given opportunities to pursue their PhDs.

Besides EPMS, independent schools also develop their own tools for assessment. For example, RGS developed a classroom observation tool to assess the teaching competency of classroom teachers. According to this tool, there is a certain benchmark score for teachers. While the benchmark is lowered for new teachers, it is higher for experienced teachers who have, for example, more than five years of teaching experience. It documents the behavior of the teacher, including relationships with the students, and lesson delivery. In addition, it also documents how the teacher performs during school functions and CCAs. As Mrs. Poh Mun See, the principal of RGS, explains:

> We do follow the MOE system for performance management. For example, we do performance planning at the beginning of the year, followed by mid-year work review, and year-end work review. This is because these are the essential steps in helping teachers understand where they are in terms of their own development and performance. But we have adapted the competency framework to suit our needs because the expectations and roles of our teachers are quite different.

This section has focused on the educative and developmental appraisal at the individual level that ensures that the quality of each teacher is continually upheld. The next section will cover the final theme of this case study to demonstrate how professional teacher learning is undertaken at the systemic level.

Professional Learning beyond Induction

Beyond the "hand holding during the first year or so" that "helps to prevent the early exit of freshly trained teachers," there is "a comprehensive framework to provide different pathways for teachers to upgrade themselves" (Goh & Lee, 2008, pp. 102, 105). The professional development of teachers is an essential aspect of the national agenda, as evidenced by the government's "move towards an all graduate recruitment by 2015" and the goal for "30% of the teaching force [to] have Master's degree qualifications by 2020" (Goodwin, 2012, p. 39). Distribution of the working hours of a Singapore teacher is shown in the following diagram (Figure 9), taken from the TALIS 2013[7] report. The report indicates that teachers spend 71% of their lesson time on actual teaching and learning (self-reported data). In addition, TALIS for 2014 (OECD, 2014b) shows that teachers in Singapore have higher than average national participation rates for a number of PD activities such as courses and workshops (93%), education conferences (61%), in-service training in external organizations (17%), network of teachers (53%), and individual and collaborative research (45%).

The actual timetable of Mdm. Rosmiliah Bte Kasmin (Figure 10), the teacher we video-recorded at Kranji Secondary School, offers a more concrete idea of how a Singapore teacher's working time is divided. Rosmiliah's timetable is very representative of the TALIS data. For example, most of her time is spent on teaching her secondary 3 and secondary 4 classes. She has a blocked time on Thursday for professional learning and development, which includes BT mentoring, professional learning communities, and Learn and Grow. She is also involved in cocurricular activities. Her administrative work is allocated in staff and department time (SDT) and department meetings (RCP). From the timetable, we can clearly see the importance of teaching and professional learning in her daily work.

All teachers are entitled to 100 hours of paid PD annually that is considered "office time" and therefore can happen during school hours with additional manpower resources provided via "relief teachers." But PD is

Figure 9. Teachers' Use of Time: Singapore-TALIS Comparison Data.

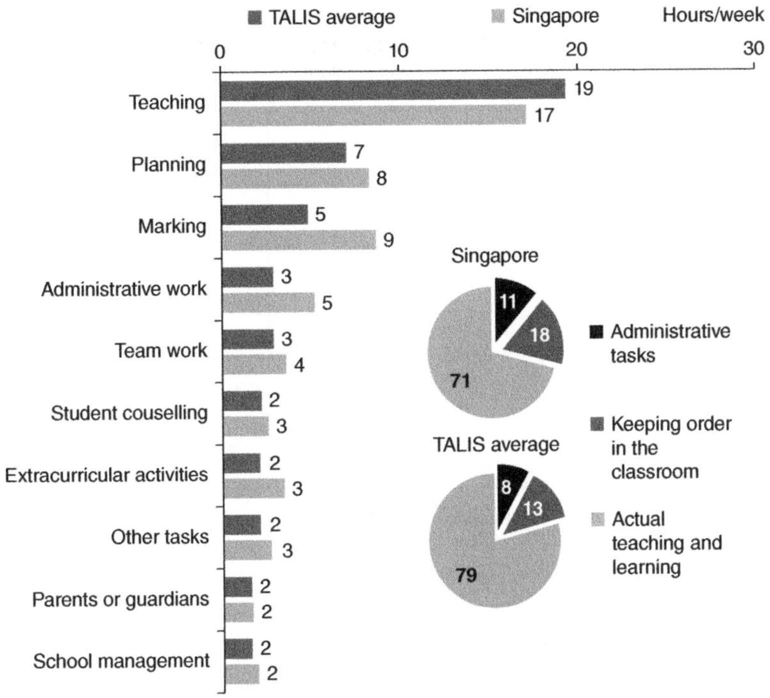
TALIS average
Singapore
Hours/week
0
10
20
30
Teaching
19
17
Planning
7
8
Marking
5
9
Administrative work
3
5
Team work
3
4
Student couselling
2
3
Extracurricular activities
2
3
Other tasks
2
3
Parents or guardians
2
2
School management
2
2
Singapore
11
18
71
TALIS average
8
13
79
Administrative tasks
Keeping order in the classroom
Actual teaching and learning

Source: OECD, 2014b, p. 3.

more than the acquisition of new skills or training, but aims to reshape the nature of teachers' work and to enhance their professionalism. Teachers have about 17 hours of timetabled teaching periods per week, as shown in the TALIS results. They can make use of their nonteaching hours to work with other teachers on lesson preparation, visit each other's classrooms to study, teaching, or engage in professional discussions and meetings with teachers from their school or across schools in learning communities. Teachers are also supported to conduct action research, lesson study, or other teacher inquiry projects in small professional learning teams. They may examine their teaching practice and student learning so as to foster more effective and innovative teaching practices, and develop curriculum resources for their departments and other teachers. Protected time is set aside in the timetable to sustain these types of collaborations. In this regard, the SSD in each school plays an

Figure 10. Mdm. Rosmiliah Bte Kasmin's Timetable in Semester 2, 2014.

(a)

Time Table 2014 Semester 2
Kranji Secondary School, Singapore
Even Week

<table>
<tr><th></th><th>Monday</th><th>Tuesday</th><th>Wednesday</th><th>Thursday</th><th>Friday</th></tr>
<tr><td>7.35 – 7.55</td><td>SDT</td><td>MA</td><td>MA</td><td>MA</td><td>MA</td></tr>
<tr><td>7.55 – 8.30</td><td>MA</td><td></td><td rowspan="2">Teaching Sec 3</td><td></td><td rowspan="2">Teaching Sec 3</td></tr>
<tr><td>8.30 – 9.00</td><td>RCP 0815 – 0850</td><td></td><td></td></tr>
<tr><td>9.00 – 9.30</td><td></td><td></td><td rowspan="2">Teaching Sec 4</td><td></td><td></td></tr>
<tr><td>9.30 – 10.00</td><td></td><td></td><td></td><td></td></tr>
<tr><td>10.00 – 10.35</td><td></td><td></td><td rowspan="2">Teaching Sec 3</td><td rowspan="2">Teaching Sec 3</td><td rowspan="2">Teaching Sec 4</td></tr>
<tr><td>10.35 – 11.05</td><td></td><td></td></tr>
<tr><td>11.05 – 11.35</td><td></td><td></td><td></td><td></td><td></td></tr>
<tr><td>11.35 – 12.05</td><td></td><td rowspan="2">Teaching Sec 4</td><td rowspan="2">Teaching Sec 4</td><td></td><td rowspan="2">Assembly CCE</td></tr>
<tr><td>12.05 – 12.35</td><td></td><td></td></tr>
<tr><td>12.35 – 13.05</td><td></td><td rowspan="2">Teaching Sec 3</td><td></td><td></td><td></td></tr>
<tr><td>13.05 – 13.35</td><td></td><td></td><td></td><td></td></tr>
<tr><td>13.35 – 14.05</td><td></td><td></td><td></td><td></td><td></td></tr>
<tr><td>14.05 – 14.35</td><td rowspan="2">Teaching Sec 3</td><td></td><td rowspan="2">Teaching Sec 4</td><td rowspan="2">Teaching Sec 4</td><td></td></tr>
<tr><td>14.35 – 15.05</td><td></td><td></td></tr>
<tr><td>15.05 – 15.35</td><td></td><td></td><td rowspan="4">CCA</td><td></td><td></td></tr>
<tr><td>15.35 – 16.05</td><td></td><td></td><td></td><td></td></tr>
<tr><td>16.05 – 16.35</td><td></td><td></td><td></td><td></td></tr>
<tr><td>16.35 – 17.05</td><td></td><td></td><td></td><td></td></tr>
</table>

important role in customizing professional learning to teacher needs and school goals. They are also in charge of planning and implementing whole-school professional learning programs with teacher leaders.

School leaders in Singapore strive to create a conducive professional learning environment for teachers. The latest TALIS results provide some concrete evidence on this area (OECD, 2014b). For example, the results show that almost all schools in Singapore provide teachers the opportunity to actively participate in decisions. In addition, 8 in 10 principals

(b)

Odd Week

	Monday	Tuesday	Wednesday	Thursday	Friday
7.35 – 7.55	SDT	MA	MA	MA	MA
7.55 – 8.30	MA	Teaching Sec 4		Teaching Sec 4	Teaching Sec 4
8.30 – 9.00	RCP 0815 - 0850				
9.00 – 9.30				Teaching Sec 4	
9.30 – 10.00					
10.00 – 10.35			Teaching Sec 3		Teaching Sec 4
10.35 – 11.05					
11.05 – 11.35					
11.35 – 12.05			Teaching Sec 4		Assembly CCE
12.05 – 12.35					
12.35 – 13.05	Teaching Sec 3	Teaching Sec 3	Teaching Sec 3	Teaching Sec 3	
13.05 – 13.35					
13.35 – 14.05					
14.05 – 14.35			Teaching Sec 4		
14.35 – 15.05					
15.05 – 15.35			CCA	L&G	
15.35 – 16.05					
16.05 – 16.35					
16.35 – 17.05					

Orange: Direct contact with students or completion of administrative work besides lesson planning and assessment

Blue: Professional learning (e.g. mentoring, professional development, PLC)

Green: Planning and assessing students' work

White: After-school hours for school-related work (e.g. preparing resources, marking)

SDT: Staff & Department Time (usually for the dissemination of information)
MA: Morning Assembly
RCP: Department Meeting (Reflection cum Planning Time)
CCA: Co-Curricular Activities
BTM: Beginning Teacher Mentoring Session (on an ad hoc basis)
PLC: Professional Learning Communities
L&G: Learn & Grow (fortnightly)

will place their emphasis on making sure teachers take responsibility for their professional learning and students' learning outcomes. From the perspective of teachers, 81% of them feel that their schools have a collaborative culture that is respectful and mutually supportive. The study also found that the collaborative professional learning culture and opportunities to participate in school decisions are positively correlated to job satisfaction.

Just as with initial teacher preparation, NIE and MOE work together synergistically to meet teachers' educational and professional needs, to support teachers' advancement, and to respond to national, as well as a plethora of ad hoc, imperatives and goals. Thus, NIE offers a variety of workshops to enhance teacher learning about the new assessments that support MOE initiatives in that direction. NIE also offers degree and diploma programs for school leaders, senior teachers, and content specialists, while the MOE has made it easier for teachers to be temporarily posted to NIE as teaching faculty for up to four years (a practice known as "secondment," which previously was only available to independent schools or the ministry), thus opening yet another PD route for teachers to learn and grow, and creating yet another mechanism for NIE and schools to be mutually informing and collaborative.

The school year in Singapore is from January to December each year. There is a total of 12 weeks of school holidays a year, which teachers can enjoy if their services are not needed during the holidays. They may use this period for overseas travel, etc. Teachers also have fully paid ordinary sick leave up to a total of 14 days in a calendar year or 60 days if he/she is warded in a hospital. Teachers are entitled to urgent private affairs leave for up to 10 working days per year. In addition, MOE has implemented other pro-family schemes such as full paid childcare leave and parent leave. The ministry also provides funding for scholarship and study leaves—both locally and abroad—facilitating teachers' movement along selected career ladders and learning along multiple dimensions. MOE's PD packages and leave scheme offer various types of scholarships, study loans, and leave provisions, which allow teachers to further their undergraduate/postgraduate studies in various areas. For instance, a teacher could take a study leave to attend university in another country or could take a study leave to intern at, for example, a local gallery to learn more about art in communities. The application for study leaves and scholarships is based on interest, experience, and merit, and there is no competition among teachers.

For example, Mdm. Rosmiliah Bte Kasmin participated in an overseas learning program in the United Kingdom, which was a three-week course on geography that combines theoretical learning and field work. The program was organized by MOE. Teachers who are interested can apply with their school leaders' recommendations. At RGS, Mrs. Mary George Cheriyan has always been interested in the principles behind policymaking and national issues. As the then director of academic studies and a member of the senior management, she was granted a scholarship and one-year study leave by RGS to pursue a master's in public administration (Link 15) at the Lee Kuan Yew School of Public Policy at the National University of Singapore. She shared with us that the learning experience helped her understand some of the key principles in policy and reform, as well as how to utilize human capital to achieve certain objectives. What she learned helped her greatly in setting up PeRL in RGS, which not only aims to support the professional learning of teachers in the school and Singapore but also aims to contribute new knowledge to the international education community. She said

> I was able to ask, what are my objectives in setting up this centre? What are some of the overarching goals? I had to view it not just as a centre within the school, but as something that can have greater impact within the fraternity in Singapore and beyond. As the Lee Kuan Yew school has a very strong Asian narrative, it is very focused on the Asia-ness of our thinking. I came back [with strong convictions] about that. One of our aspirations of PeRL is to cultivate an Asian discourse on education.

A series of system-wide strategies were also established to attain the vision of teacher-led professional learning. First, platforms for teacher-leaders to lead professional learning were created via subject chapters, professional networks, professional focus groups, and professional learning communities. Teacher leaders support teachers' professional learning within and beyond the schools to the entire teaching fraternity. There are three essential aspects in the role that teacher leaders play: (1) pedagogical leaders, (2) instructional mentors, and (3) professional learning leaders. As pedagogical leaders, they are experts in the teaching and learning of their subject disciplines; as instructional mentors, they facilitate the development of less effective teachers so as to help them become more effective; as professional learning leaders, they plan and facilitate professional learning activities for teachers in the fraternity. For example, professional learning communities are set up and led by teacher leaders to facilitate teacher collaboration focusing on pedagogical innovation and subject mastery.

Second, strong organizational structures for professional learning were developed, among which are training entitlements for teachers; funding for MOE-organized courses; timetabled protected time for teachers to engage in lesson planning, reflection, and PD activities; and an online portal providing one-stop access to learning, collaboration, and resources for all MOE staff.

Third, a number of initiatives to preserve and grow the values, beliefs, and practices of the teaching profession were introduced. The Ethos of the Teaching Profession was established and the MOE Heritage Centre was set up so that a slice of the past could be displayed to remind and inspire teachers. Awards and recognition for teachers were also created to recognize role models in education.

Among the many investments is the Teachers' Network, so named in 1998 by MOE as part of the TSLN initiative. The mission of the Teachers' Network is to serve as a catalyst and support for teacher-initiated development through sharing, collaboration, and reflection. The Teachers' Network was reconceptualized to be AST in 2009. AST was started to spearhead the PD of Singapore teachers. It was envisioned to be the home of the teaching profession and help catalyze teacher capacity-building. The AST mission is to build "a teacher-led culture of professional excellence centered on the holistic development of the child" (AST, n.d.c.).

AST was founded to also pull the master teachers together to support their learning and to enable them to organize professional learning for others. There are currently 76 master teachers and principal master teachers in the academies and language centers.

Ms. Cynthia Seto, a principal master teacher for mathematics currently assigned to AST, shared her view of the academy's role as facilitating the spread of good practice:

> I see the set-up of Academy of Singapore Teachers as encouraging teachers to take ownership and teacher leadership of their professional development. It provides opportunities for teachers to collaborate, to interact with teachers from other schools. I was a senior teacher for seven years before I became a master teacher. In my previous school, there were three senior teachers, including me. Although we worked together in mentoring teachers, we were from different subjects. The opportunity to interact with senior teachers teaching the same subject is important to deepen our pedagogical content knowledge and teaching practices. I feel that the academy is well situated to bring about this kind of collaboration, to spread good practices across schools.
>
> Right now, my first goal as a master teacher is to raise the professional standards of the mathematics chapter. . .To do that, we conduct workshops [and] provide an opportunity for workshop follow-up for sustained learning. . . I see myself as a catalyst to encourage teachers to form networked learning communities (NLCs) for us to talk further about what we are doing, for everyone to reflect

on our practice, and to share effective strategies to meet the diverse learning needs. We want our students to learn mathematics with understanding.

We could come together to co-design a lesson and then look at how it works in the classroom. After the lesson observation by teachers, we will reflect and discuss. It may not be a perfect lesson, but it's an opportunity for learning. Teachers [may say], "Hey, I'm going to do something like that in my own class," and then they'll bring it back to try in their own class. It could be in the form of a video, it could be in the form of a student artifact. . . It is encouraging to hear teachers saying "Oh, my students, this is what they have done. Oh, your school does this like that? Mine is like that. Oh, we could do something, you know?"

With regard to AST's vision of shaping a teacher-led culture of professional excellence, Ms. Irene Tan, who is also a principal master teacher at AST, shared how teacher leadership is emerging:

When we first started the academy, we wanted to create a teacher-led culture to raise the professional standard. Because of the fact that we are master teachers, we are expected to lead the chapter. We are trying to also empower the next level, which is the core team members. We have a subject chapter led by master teachers, then we have the core team. The core team is made up of senior teachers and lead teachers from different zones (north, south, east, west). In my team, we have ten of us.

Previously, my colleague and I, who is also a master teacher, were leading and planning. Starting this year, 2013, I actually see that the [core team members] are taking the lead. They are the ones who say that, "Irene, besides doing this, can we consider also to share with the beginning teachers, for example, how to conduct a chemistry practical lesson properly?" Because when they come in, one of the biggest learning gaps is that they're not confident to bring a class of 40 students into a chemistry lab. It's a little scary and daunting for them because of all the chemicals and the classroom management and the potential safety issue, so they're a little scared. The senior teachers have come together and they volunteered to do zonal workshops. They'll sit down and plan. Come next month in November, my colleague and I will help look through the workshop material and then we'll give them the full support.

They are the ones who identified the learning area for other teachers and they're planning these things for the teachers. I see that teacher leadership coming up very strongly. Science experiments is

> not the only area they have identified. One group will look at misconceptions in chemistry and they would like to use lesson study to try it out. Another group is looking at helping teachers look at item setting for database questions, for example. That is for the chemistry syllabus. They are trying to involve senior teachers beyond the core team. We're reaching out to the second tier.

Together with the emerging teacher-led culture of professional learning is the change in teachers' views on teacher leadership and their increasingly strong identity of being teacher leaders. Ms. Cynthia Seto and Ms. Irene Tan shared with us:

> The teachers gave feedback to me that they're more confident, especially the senior teachers, because the PD activities are very practice-based. At the same time, it's very relevant to their role and to their classroom teaching. With the support given, they are more confident, and they know that if there's anything that they are unsure about, they know where they'll go to. That is important. They get affirmation from their fellow colleagues, as well as from the academy itself.
>
> With the setup of AST, they have more opportunities to play their role as a teacher leader and also to reach out to play a more significant role in the professional development of teachers and be able to talk with colleagues. So they find that there is something they enjoy and they feel that they are contributing, they are being part of that community. I think the sense of community is stronger now.
>
> The identity of the idea of senior teacher [is stronger now]: the lead teachers also see themselves as teacher leaders. For the longest time, the term teacher leader usually referred to heads of department and vice principals who are in-school leaders. [Senior teachers] see themselves as teacher leaders now. Not only we [at the AST] give them a platform to share with other teachers, one of the things that we consciously look into is to build the capacity of this group of senior teachers as well. As they help others grow, they themselves will grow.

In addition to AST, other academies and language centers were also set up to support subject-specific professional learning. The Physical Education and Sports Teacher Academy (PESTA) and the Singapore Teachers' Academy for the aRts (STAR) both support teacher learning in those subjects, plus the English Language Institute of Singapore (ELIS) provides PD for English Language teachers; additionally, the Malay Language Centre of Singapore (MLCS), the Singapore Centre for Chinese Language (SCCL) and the Umar Pulavar Tamil Language Centre (UPTLC) support development for Malay, Chinese, and Tamil language teachers. To support PD planning for in-service teachers, the Teacher Growth Model (TGM) was developed as a learning framework with desired teacher outcomes (Figure 11). The TGM learning continuum is organized according to five teacher outcomes: the ethnical educator; the competent professional; the collaborative learner; the transformational leader; and the community builder. Under each teacher outcome are the skills and competencies required for growth and development so that teachers can achieve all five teacher outcomes. Teachers also use TGM to examine their professional learning needs. Learning programs and activities are themed according to each outcome and competency. Teachers can choose the area that they want to enhance and participate in the corresponding professional learning programs targeted at that area. Learning and development occurs in a variety of modes, such as courses, mentoring, e-learning, learning journeys, reflective practice, and research-based practice.

Figure 11. Teacher Growth Model.

Source: MOE, 2012b.

Professional learning activities (Link 16) are centered around providing holistic programs and environments to facilitate the holistic development of the students along multiple dimensions, including the cognitive, physical, social, moral, and ethical dimensions. As the key to successful facilitation of students' holistic development, teachers' professional learning is one of the most important priorities on school agendas. Schools strive to build a strong culture of professional learning, manifested through various professional learning activities such as SMP and professional learning communities. The following are some noticeable highlights in terms of PD.

1. *Research and Teacher Inquiry*

As practitioners, almost all teachers are involved in research and innovation projects examining their teaching and learning to better meet the needs of students. Teachers are not only supposed to be competent in teaching, but also to become reflective practitioners through research and co-learning. Schools provide structured time for teachers to come together as a group to discuss and implement their projects. Teachers may choose to use a variety of teacher inquiry approaches—action research, lesson study, learning study, and learning circle—to investigate their practices. To facilitate teachers' development of research competence, support from internal and external educational experts is provided for teachers. Over the years, teachers' skills in terms of using research to gather data and evidence to make informed decisions have grown. Research findings are also shared through various platforms at the departmental and school levels, other local schools, and local and international conferences. Each year, the school may have different topics and areas as the research focus, topics which are collaboratively identified by the senior management and teachers as a whole. When teachers feel that the structured time is not enough to discuss their projects, they will come together on their own initiative whenever they feel it is needed, either within the school day or after it. The research projects are not only done at a subject level, but also go beyond specific subjects to involve collaboration among different departments and disciplines. It is important to note that while a significant proportion of teachers do research, others are doing smaller or developmental projects that may not involve a full-blown research protocol but are nevertheless designed to collect evidence to support the improvement of their teaching and learning.

Ms. Tan Hwee Pin, the principal of Kranji Secondary School, shared with us how research is highlighted and encouraged in professional learning(Link 17):

> All our teachers have to come together to work on a research project where they get together in small groups to solve a teaching and learning issue—it can take the form of a lesson study, action research, or innovation project. We set aside structured time for the groups and they have one year to complete the project. At the end of it, each group will have to present their project to fellow colleagues during Staff Innovation Day. We invite professional judges to select the best entries, and we have seen a couple of great ideas emerge from this exercise. I believe that this research process motivates our teachers to be more reflective and critical of their practice and strategies.

Mdm. Rosmiliah Bte Kasmin and her team from Kranji Secondary School embarked on an action research project in 2014, where they looked at the effectiveness of using a particular ICT tool in teaching. This project compared two groups of students: one group was exposed to the ICT tool, whereas the other was exposed to the typical way of teaching. From this project, the team was able to explore the use of the new ICT tool to facilitate teaching and learning. The evidence gathered from student surveys indicated that students found the ICT lessons more engaging and fun. The use of the ICT tool also allows students to do more in-depth study around the concepts and relationships they are learning.

Teachers are well supported by the schools to conduct research projects, not only in terms of resources and methodology, but also in terms of dissemination of research results in different platforms. As Mr. Azahar Bin Mohamed Noor at RGS explained:

> On top of the opportunities to attend workshops, there are opportunities to attend conferences or even to present papers at international conferences. These presentations involve teachers at RGS doing their own research or research on program evaluation. It is supported by PeRL in RGS, where they have expert teachers to guide us in terms of how do to research. When teachers propose a research project, they will assign one expert for teachers to get feedback and alternate views.

Emphasizing the importance of research to a teacher, Mr. Azahar Bin Mohamed Noor added, "This is not just about being a competent teacher, but also about the teacher as an inquirer and reflective practitioner of their own craft."

The professional learning of teachers impacts not only teachers' professional growth but also students' future learning experiences. The following vignette of Mr. Azahar Bin Mohamed Noor's practitioner inquiry (PI) project demonstrates how teacher professional learning and students' learning can be seamlessly connected. Practitioner inquiry in RGS is based on a shared vision of knowledge creation and sharing at the school and the aim of improving teaching and learning (Tan, 2015).

Portrait of Practice

At a feedback meeting, Mr. Azahar Bin Mohamed Noor presented his PI research on the Regional Immersion and Community Exploration (RICE) Program for year 2 students at RGS. He is the leader of the program team that developed and implemented the RICE program. Through visits to cities and places overseas, RICE aims to develop students in a number of areas: (1) global mindset, (2) sociocultural intelligence, (3) citizenship, and (4) reflective disposition. His research has two main purposes. First, it aims to evaluate the extent to which these goals were achieved. Second, it aims to assess the planning and implementation processes to sieve out areas that were successful and those that need further improvement.

About 10 of his colleagues in RGS formed the audience of the feedback session, including research experts from PeRL and his colleagues who participated in the RICE program. After consolidating the feedback from this meeting, the results will be presented to the vice principal in charge of the program for approval. The results of the project and recommendations for improvement will then be presented to the senior management before the program team implements and actualizes the recommendations in the next round of RICE.

Mr. Azahar Bin Mohamed Noor's presentation began with his understanding of the essence of PI, which demonstrates his clear understanding of the purpose of doing PI and the requirements of conducting a PI that is meaningful to teachers and the students. "There must be rigor in the data—the evidence that we collect, how we analyze the data and how it impacts on our programs."

However, teachers also shared that the biggest challenge of conducting research is time. As a result, teachers have to also utilize their own time for collaborative work and research, which in a way reflects Singapore teachers' devotedness and professionalism.

2. Sharing of Expertise and Knowledge

Teacher leaders in the school conduct workshops to share teaching strategies. They use concrete examples to explain and model the strategies. Teachers attending these sharings discuss and reflect on the usefulness of these strategies in their own classrooms and how they can customize them for their own students and subjects. Through this, the entire fraternity can be exposed to new ideas and strategies, which ultimately benefit students' learning. As commented by a teacher we interviewed, "when the teachers learn new skills and try out new activities and pedagogy, it would actually allow the students to be more engaged in class and even get a different perspective of understanding."

Portrait of Practice

Kranji Secondary School has a professional learning session called Learn and Grow, which takes place every alternative week. One of the activities in Learn and Grow is the skillful teacher workshops conducted by senior teachers who rotate their roles. Mdm. Rosmiliah Bte Kasmin shared with us what this activity is about:

> We package it in a manner that we bring the teachers on a learning journey of the new pedagogical skills, based on the skillful teachers' book. What we do is we select certain skills we would like to share with teachers. Three senior teachers will work together as a team and read up on that particular skill. They will explain to the teachers what the skill is all about. On top of that, rather than just explain the skills, we use examples or activities that we use in class to exemplify to the teachers how we actually carry out these skills in class. We get the teachers to do a bit of reflection and discussion with their partner about the activity and what they want to embark on when they go back to classroom. A teacher sharing is conducted after the activity.

Mdm. Rosmiliah Bte Kasmin stressed the purpose of the skillful teacher workshop, which is for teachers to learn and renew their pedagogical skills.

> Being a teacher, if you continue doing things the way you do every time, without knowing other different ways to do, you may become boring and your students may not find your lessons engaging. So we are giving teachers a platform and opportunity just to

> talk about new ideas or even sharing things that may or may not have worked in their classes. At least these things create a forum of sharing for the teachers as well.

She further points out that the workshops also make the learning of pedagogical skills easy and practical.

> The skillful teacher workshop lasts for about 15–20 minutes. We do not want to make it very long and draggy, but make it short and impactful. The most important is that the teachers can get the ideas. We try to do bite-sized skills rather than doing many. Therefore, we only select certain skills for a particular session.

While senior teachers and master teachers play an important role in teacher capacity building within schools, their PD is also well taken care of by the system. One important platform is the cluster system of schools, which normally has about 10–13 schools, across levels (primary, secondary, and junior college). The cluster system provides a professional learning platform for teacher leaders that can help to build their leadership capacity so that they can, in turn, build the capacity of teachers in their schools. Ms. Irene Tan, a chemistry teacher and now a principal master teacher with AST, used to work in the cluster system of schools. She explained:

> In my cluster, I had 13 schools and my office was in one of the schools. I had the autonomy to work with the teachers as well as the heads of department and the vice principals in areas that they wanted me to look into: for example, mentoring or hand-holding the new key personnel, because I was a head of department for 13 years before I became a master teacher.
>
> I also worked with the experienced teachers as well as senior teachers. I belonged to the senior teacher guild in my cluster. [This is] where all the senior teachers in the cluster will come together. They usually have a chairman to head the professional learning so they will chart out the year's learning.
>
> For example, they will organize for each other one or two learning journeys, some sharing sessions, and workshops where they will invite others to come in. Basically, they look at their own learning needs. For example, if this year the guild feels that most of our senior teachers are very interested in looking at assessment, they'll try and source for a speaker or somebody relevant to run a workshop for the senior teachers. As they build their own capacity, they can then share this knowledge and experience with the new teachers in their school.

3. Create, Implement, and Review Cycle

The school professional learning activities follow a cycle where teachers collaboratively create and design the strategies they are going to use in the classroom, and then implement them in their classrooms, followed by reviewing the implementation and making improvements for the next implementation. This particular cycle enables teachers to get together and consider lesson innovations, and talk about the impact of their practices on students. It enables continuous improvement based on evidence gathered from students' responses. For example, as Mr. Azahar Bin Mohamed Noor described:

> About five or six years ago, we introduced something called article analysis, where students have to critique an article. We realised that it was a big jump for the students. For the last two years, my team and I have used a new assessment for article analysis. We use argument mapping in which students have to read and map the argument first, before they evaluate an argument in an article. This is an example of the cycle of designing implementing and reviewing. This whole process allows our teachers to have a sense of ownership and autonomy.

Teachers in RGS continuously create and experiment with their teaching. Mr. Azahar Bin Mohamed Noor shared with us how his team has implemented a new tool in their teaching and how that brings them enjoyment:

> We discussed in our last Professional Learning Space (PLS) about portfolios. The good thing is that the team thinks, "Let's do it. Let's find out more about how portfolio looks like, and maybe this year we can experiment." That's something that I really enjoy here, because you can experiment. If it doesn't work, it's okay. We get the team on board to work on it.

4. Collective Responsibility

The professional learning activities are intended to involve the entire faculty in the school, from the principal and senior management, to each and every teacher. In other words, it is not just teachers who will sit down to discuss their lessons, but members from senior management will sit down with teachers as peers to listen, discuss, share their experiences and ideas, and contribute their expertise. The dedicated time for professional learning and the involvement of senior management greatly encourage the teachers to take these learning opportunities seriously.

Mr. Azahar Bin Mohamed Noor talked about how RGS school management emphasize professional learning:

> What I like is that when we have a dedicated time, it's a message that the time for Professional Learning Space (PLS) is important. I must say that the senior management take the PLS sessions very seriously. They join us, even the principals. They take it seriously, and we take it seriously as well.

Mrs. Mary Cheriyan elaborated on how the school takes professional learning as a collective responsibility (Link 18):

> PLS is collective responsibility. During this time, the entire faculty—right up to the principal, the entire senior management is involved. It is not just teachers who will be sitting down to discuss the lessons. I will sit down with teachers as peers to discuss what are some suitable strategies, what worked, what didn't, and bring whatever I can contribute.

The collaboration among teachers often goes beyond departmental level boundaries. Mr. Azahar Bin Mohamed Noor told us about a project in RGS involving the collaboration of three departments—English, Social Studies, and Philosophy:

> We want the girls to be an advocate and an active citizen. So we decided to introduce a project called the advocacy project for active citizens. It was a collaborative project among three departments including English, Social Studies, and Philosophy. The girls will undertake an advocacy project. They were assessed by three different departments. The language department will look at their use of language in terms of how persuasive they were in their advocacy speech; the Social Studies department will look at their thinking process, their process of advocacy and research; the Philosophy department will look at what are the questions they use.

Besides conducting research, different departments also meet to discuss other issues concerning teaching and learning.

Portrait of Practice

PLS is not just limited to subjects. Sometimes we collaborate with the Philosophy department to look at the art of questioning. Sometimes we have a meeting together with the English department, because we feel that students' writings are not clear and precise enough. These things will happen along the way. Even for their research skills, if we find they are not able to be self-reliant on their research skills, we will give feedback to the research department and see what intervention they can implement.

Mr. Azahar Bin Mohamed Noor, teacher, RGS

Portrait of Practice

What happens in our PLS is that every Friday during 2pm–4pm curriculum time, in all departments, teachers meet together. PLS follows the particular cycle "create, implement, review." For example, we create a lesson, design the unit and the strategies we are going to use, and then implement in the classroom. In creating the lesson, you discuss it during the PLS in terms of how this lesson is going to be carried out, what are my big ideas, etc. Then we will implement it in the classroom. For the next PLS, we talk about what happened in the classroom, how students behaved, what worked, what didn't work. Then you review it. So this particular cycle enables teachers to get together, collaborate, and talk about the impact of their lessons on the classroom.

Mrs. Mary Cheriyan, director of PeRL, RGS

5. Networked Learning Communities

Networked learning communities (NLCs) are platforms offered by AST where teachers across schools come together to learn and work collaboratively on professional areas of interest. For example, there are NLCs (1) that are subject- or role-specific (e.g., NLCs of SSDs; NLCs of allied educators), (2) that cater to specific interests (e.g., an NLC of inquiry into lesson study).

Ms. Irene Tan described how academy leaders help organize other lead teachers from the field by subject area and how workshops are designed to create applications to practice.

> Basically, in a subject chapter, the senior teachers who represent the different zones will come for meetings and consultation with us. Then we find out from them what their learning needs are before we even conceptualize and mount any workshop. We hear from the senior teachers, "Oh, my BTs actually need these areas of training." Then that's where we come together and then we design workshops for them. . . Where possible, teacher PD should be just in time and

> sustained and on the job, so that's why we are working through the senior teachers.
>
> The way we design our workshop, we affectionately call it a five C approach to teacher PD. The first C is actually curiosity. That is to pique the teacher's sense of curiosity to want to know more about the workshop. The second C is about comprehension. It's to get the teachers to understand and know about the new pedagogy or teaching strategies. The third one is to convince. During the workshop, we will try to share with the teachers not just how it is done, but why it should be done that way and what are some success stories to try and convince the teacher that this is the way indeed to go forward. The fourth is contextualization. We give teachers the opportunity to work on something. Let's say they come for a PBL workshop and during the day, we will give the teachers time to work in team to craft a problem scenario and prepare the lesson, so that when they go back to the school, they can actually carry out the lesson plan or the unit plan with their students. The last C is "change practice." Then, they always come back for a celebration, so that's [an additional] C. When they come together, they will present their teaching ideas and then how they have tried it out with the students and what are some of the learning points. What do they see in their students and how do they feel as a teacher after carrying out the whole thing and whether or not this can be sustainable in their point of view.

A typical NLC that is based on teachers' specific interest is one on lesson study. Teachers can refine their lesson study practice with help from their teacher leaders in schools (i.e., senior and lead teachers) and master teachers at AST. Ms. Irene Tan and Ms. Cynthia Seto together described how teachers are supported to learn lesson study through workshops and networked learning community:

> For lesson study [workshops], we encourage schools to send a group of at least three teachers so that they have each other's support during the journey. There are usually three to four face-to-face sessions in the lesson study workshop. The workshops are usually conducted in a blended manner where resources and reading materials are placed in an online learning platform. The teachers can then read and participate in discussions on the online forums. This will provide the teachers with some idea of what lesson study is and for them to have a professional discourse.
>
> The first face-to-face session is where we facilitate the learning of the what and why of lesson study as well as how the research lessons can be designed. In the second session, they go more in-depth into the lesson design and planning. The teachers are also given ample

> opportunities to provide feedback to each other. We then refine the lesson plan and one of the teachers will teach it with the rest observing in a classroom. The lesson observation is the third session of a typical workshop. The master teachers facilitate both the pre- and post-lesson discussions so that the teachers can observe how facilitation is carried out. In the fourth face-to-face session, all participants come back and share their lesson study experience in terms of planning, implementation, and learning (both students' and teachers').
>
> And, we do not stop there. We encourage them to form a lesson study NLC. The NLC [offers] a more fluid approach in the sense that the members will direct what, when and how they want to do. The NLC members plan lessons together and they can conduct the research lessons in their respective schools or they visit one of the member's classroom to observe the lesson.

6. *A Discipline-specific Approach*

Another area that impressed the research team of the Singapore approach to professional learning is the emphasis on a discipline-specific approach that develops pedagogical content knowledge. From Ms. Irene Tan:

> More often than not, the teachers will continue with lesson study . . . in their own department. One of the reasons I see this [is that] our lesson study approach has not been in a generic manner. When we conduct these series of workshops, like four afternoons for the teacher, we do it by subject. For example, if I do a lesson study workshop, it's for chemistry teachers only. Cynthia would do [a workshop] for elementary maths teachers. The conversation is very rich in terms of content.
>
> [We rely on] the signature pedagogy that comes with this particular subject: maths has a way to teach mathematics. Science, there's a way to teach science. It is very different from the generic one way when they just talk about lesson study. Then they may not have the opportunity to go very deep into the content. For us in AST, we have the luxury of a few of us all doing lesson study. Then we can really tailor the discussion to the subject.

7. *Ample Professional Learning Opportunities beyond School*

Teachers are encouraged to pursue professional learning beyond their school boundaries based on their interests and passion. For example, they may apply for no-pay leave to pursue their masters. Teachers can also go for workshops or conferences outside the school.

8. Cultivating an Asian Perspective

Many teachers in Singapore are cognizant of the limitations of theories and practices in Western countries and aspire to cultivate a confident Asian discourse on education. This is one of the important aspirations of PeRL at RGS.

Professional Perspective

One of our aspirations of PeRL is to cultivate an Asian discourse on education. Our center is organizing a symposium in two weeks' time. We want teachers from other schools to come in and generate discourse through research, sharing, or whatever. The idea is that we cultivate a confident Asian perspective to education, because a lot of the things we have done are taken from the West with certain assumptions. And I'm already questioning those assumptions—do they necessarily work? Are they universal? Do they necessarily work in a Singapore context? In our school context, those are some of the assumptions I have been able to have the confidence to question.

Mrs. Mary Cheriyan, director of PeRL, RGS

9. A Systemic Approach

One highlight of the systemic approach is the role of the SSD. Every school has an SSD, an equivalent to a head of department, whose job is to ensure that the training and professional development programs are customized to the needs of the teachers in school and support the school's goals. The SSD, in consultation with the school leaders, is in charge of drawing up a whole-school staff development plan and also working with individual teachers to draw up their own training plans. The SSD also taps the expertise of the teacher leaders to facilitate teacher learning through mentoring, formal courses, and learning communities. Therefore, the SSD plays an important role in helping every teacher progress continually in her/his professional development and establishing a culture of collaborative learning to achieve the desired school outcomes.

A second highlight in the systemic approach is that the professional learning is holistic and systematic at both the school level and the individual staff level. For example, in RGS, every year there will be a total professional learning plan for each staff including teaching, nonteaching, and key personnel. Their professional learning activities are differentiated according to their own needs. Professional learning is not a one-week or one-month event, but an ongoing process throughout the year. Every year there is a different focus, for example, critical thinking, infusing ICT into classroom, or formative assessment. However, different topics from year to year are not separated, but integrated in the sense that when new topics are introduced, the former topics will still be present in professional learning activities in one way or another. In addition, former foci and topics will be put into the appraisal processes of teachers.

10. Student-Centered Professional Learning

The design of professional learning opportunities is student-centered. Given this philosophy of catering to students' needs, teachers are not afraid of asking themselves difficult questions. One important question that teachers ask is "What is my contribution to students' learning?" Student feedback is often sought to review the teaching and learning processes. (Link 19) For example, at one professional learning session that the research team attended at RGS, the Social Studies department was discussing students' complaint about having too much reading. Mr. Azahar Bin Mohamed Noor shared with us how RGS engages students in giving feedback to the school:

> The school engages the students in terms of teaching and learning, CCAs, and other issues. There is a student body called the "Congress," which gets feedback from the student body. It is quite common that students' feedback is channeled to the congress, where some of the students' feedback will be conveyed to the school management. The school management will then inform the staff. And we will discuss the students' feedback at the teachers' level. So there's a lot of dialogue and engagement with students with regard to our programs and policies. Another channel of feedback is the survey with students. This is called the RGS experiential survey, where students give feedback to the teachers teaching them directly. It is done twice a year. Through this, we get feedback on whether they enjoyed their learning, and whether they were sufficiently challenged.

11. Finding Time

Teaching is becoming an increasingly challenging profession. Together with various kinds of educational reforms and initiatives, it is common that teachers are taking on more and more responsibilities and heavier workloads. To ensure effective professional learning, it is of critical importance that schools structure protected time for teachers to learn. The school leaders in Singapore are well aware of this. Ms. Irene Tan shared with us the approach of the school where she was formerly posted:

> From the school I came from, we used to have weekly contact time with the staff. What we did was, we didn't use the contact time to do administrative things. We tried to convert the contact time, which is usually about two hours per week, into professional learning time. Besides that one hour timetabled time, we have two more hours freed up because the school leader felt that, "Well, some of these things I can communicate through emails and though electronic means."
>
> So we can creatively cut down some things to create time for teachers to come together. But the timetabled part is good because during curriculum time, we can have a time slot for all the teachers in the team to meet. In a sense, it is good because we know for sure that on this weekday at this time, say Wednesday 10:00am, we are all free for that one hour. If we really want to do a research lesson for our lesson study, we can actually go into a class and conduct [the lesson] and we know that we are all free during that period.

Professional Development along Differentiated Career Tracks

In tandem with the wide range of PD opportunities open to teachers, there are clearly differentiated career tracks that allow for career progression along the areas of strength displayed by each teacher. The concept of a teacher's career ladder is well developed in Singapore, offering teachers different routes for advancement and leadership. While the traditional role of the principal as the main school leader still predominates, leadership has become a much more distributed concept where it is being devolved or shared across the institution (Spillane, 2005). MOE developed Edu-Pac (Education Service Professional Development and Career Plan) (Link 20) "for teachers to develop their potential to the fullest" (MOE, 2009).

An examination of these many pathways reveals that they take into account the fact that among "the full complement of 33,000 teachers. . . a quarter of our teachers are below the age of 30 and have less than 5 years of experience" (Heng, 2012), and therefore would seek and/or need very different kinds of opportunities to lead, than might experienced teachers. The notion of multiple pathways also aligns with a "person-centric"

stance toward education reform whereby the aim is to develop to the fullest all teachers' capacities according to their unique talents and proclivities, so as to fully capitalize upon their skills and knowledge and utilize them in the service of school improvement and the enhancement of classroom practice. Finally, multiple pathways help to sustain and retain veteran teachers by offering them different avenues and programs for developing their skills and deepening their knowledge such that they can be prepared for meaningful leadership opportunities commensurate with their experience and skill. These pathways fall into three categories: the university-based pathway; the school-based pathway; the ministry-based pathway, each of which is described in greater detail below.

The university-based pathway is a familiar route to advancement and further develops the knowledge and skills of educators through additional preparation and coursework at the postgraduate level. Singapore has created several such pathways that bring NIE in collaboration with MOE and AST to support the continuous education of teachers and school middle leaders.

To encourage teachers to stay relevant and updated in content and pedagogy, MOE collaborated with NIE and created the Professional Development Continuum Model (PDCM) in 2005. PDCM provides graduate teachers with an alternative pathway to a master's degree while working as a full-time teacher. The scheme was enhanced in August 2012, and it is now called the Enhanced PDCM. For teachers who are accepted into the Enhanced PDCM, MOE will subsidize the minimum number of courses required for graduation. Teachers will need to make a one-time payment during matriculation. Upon completion of the program, teachers are required to serve a one-year bond with MOE from the conferment date (NIE, n.d.b.).

In July 2007, NIE launched the Management and Leadership in Schools Program (MLS). It is designed as a full-time 17-week in-service program meant specially for middle-level leaders, who are already heads of departments. The selection of these leaders is made by the school principal and cluster superintendent. Upon enrollment into the program, participants have their fees fully borne by MOE and still continue to receive their monthly salaries.

MLS is distinguished by a deliberate integration of theory and practice, as well as attention to "glocal" issues, both the global and the local. Alongside a rigorous academic component, participants undertake a project that engages them in authentic learning experiences. In the project, they can put into practice what they have learned in the theoretical components of their leadership modules. Group work is also an inherent trait of the program where participants are asked, in groups, to conceptualize a one-year curriculum that tries out an innovative practice or initiates change in a local school, taking into account the specific needs and context of that school. A key feature of the program is the overseas and industrial trips. Participants are given an opportunity to visit a country within the Asia-Pacific region in order to study its education system. While there, they also visit the local industries of that country and are provided with the opportunity to observe the operational workings of the chosen organizations. The main aim from these visits is to offer participants alternative exposure to education systems and the running of different organizations. This is an example of a university-based executive program for middle-level leaders who are already engaged in leadership work and school-based reform at their schools.

Other examples include the Leaders in Education Programme, where NIE "works in partnership with the ministry to provide a development platform that prepares educational leaders for the challenges and demands of a fast-changing system" (NIE, n.d.a.), as well as programs for senior teachers to enable them "to achieve the vision of innovating in the classroom and school, in their roles as instructional leaders and coaches to younger colleagues" (NIE, n.d.f.). Additionally, AST and NIE collaborate to conduct leadership programs for "teacher-leaders on the teaching track (appointed senior teachers, lead teachers and master teachers)" in "an integrated continual series of three milestones programmes" (AST, 2012). These programs are titled the Teacher Leaders Programme, all designed to "reflect the teacher-leaders' expected scope of influence" (AST, 2012) and hone their capacities as educational innovators, and become expert guides and mentors to their peers. While each of these leadership programs may target a different audience, they are all "future-oriented, with an emphasis on leadership capability in a dynamic and complex context" (NIE, n.d.a.).

The school-based pathway is Singapore's response to the common characterization of teaching as a "flat career" (Danielson, 2007; Goodlad & McMannon, 2004), whereby the role and work of veteran teachers differ hardly from that of fresh novices, and that if teachers want to advance, they typically have to leave the classroom. Of course this situation has changed somewhat given the expanding definitions of leadership and increased understanding that teachers can—and should—lead *from* the classroom. Still, the notion of a career ladder for teachers, one of the hallmarks of the nearly three-decades-old Holmes Group report (1986), has remained a contentious and ill-defined idea, especially given its attachment to merit pay, which always raises the question of how merit can, or ought to, be measured.

In Singapore, the complex performance appraisal system in place is designed to operationalize "merit" and concretize what teachers need to accomplish in order to be deemed "meritorious." Earlier, we have already described the holistic appraisal system known as EPMS. A deeper examination of this appraisal system reveals a synergistic relationship between teachers' performance appraisals and leadership pathways open to them. Thus, strong performance is typically tied to forward movement along three leadership trajectories, namely the teaching track, the leadership track, and the senior specialist track (see Figure 12). Teachers are all assessed by the EPMS system, which has customized standards for each of the career tracks.

Each of these tracks includes deep levels of expertise, accomplishment, and experience within a particular domain, and each level of expertise typically represents yet another (expanded) opportunity to lead and exert influence over a particular sphere. Leadership within the school is clearly valued. Those aspiring to advance within the teaching track must meet the criteria spelled out for the positions. These standards are assessed through a professional portfolio, which includes a personal statement on taking up the higher appointment, a summary of evidence satisfying each accreditation standard, and supporting data to substantiate the evidence (e.g., lesson plans, presentations).

The standards build on teaching evaluation criteria such as holistic development of pupils through quality learning, pastoral care and well-being, and cocurricular activities, and the criteria become broader

Figure 12. Different Career Tracks for Teachers.

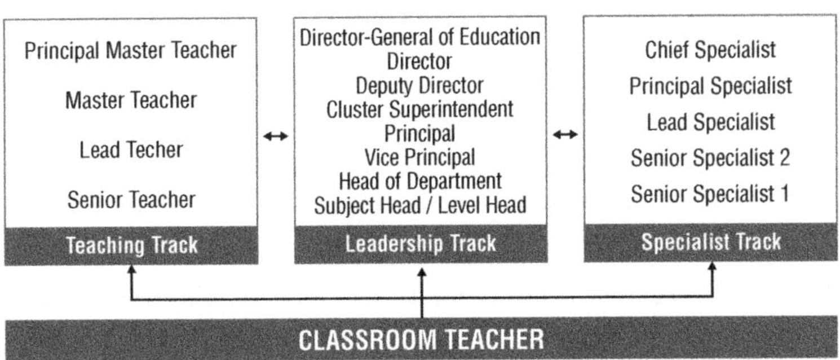

Source: MOE, n.d.b.

as the teacher advances to the next level. These include contributions to the school, cluster, zone, and nation; collaboration and networking; and contributions to a culture of professionalism, ethos, and standards. Through the teaching track, teachers can aspire first to be senior teachers, then they can move on to become lead teachers, and then progress further to the level of master teachers and principal master teachers. As they advance up the teaching track, they assume teacher leadership roles within their school or the larger teaching fraternity, serving as instructional, pedagogical leaders, and professional learning leaders. Master teachers move to the respective academies (e.g., ELIS) and are not sited in schools. This track has just been recently augmented to include "a new super scale-grade principal master teacher position as the apex of the teaching track and the creation of a new position of a lead teacher in schools" (Lee & Tan, 2010, p. 2).

The story of Ms. Cynthia Seto, a principal master teacher for mathematics currently assigned to AST, exemplifies the career progression for teachers in the teaching track. At the academy, she designs and supports PD for other teachers and teacher leaders. She described how she came to this post as she moved along the career ladder:

> I was a teacher leader. I moved from a classroom teacher to become a senior teacher. [As a] senior teacher, you have teaching periods, just like any teachers, except that you may have one to three periods fewer than other classroom teachers so that you have time for mentoring. A main responsibility of a senior teacher is to help the beginning teachers, as well as more experienced ones who aspire to be a teacher leader.
>
> Then from a senior teacher, I moved on to become a master teacher. When I decided to send my portfolio for the appointment to be master teacher, I was very clear that my passion is to build teachers' capacity in the teaching of mathematics.
>
> To be considered for appointment as master teachers, we need to be nominated by the principals. Once we are shortlisted, we will then work on our portfolio. In our portfolio, we are assessed under three standards, which cover student outcomes, professional outcomes, and organizational outcomes. Finally, we are interviewed by a selection panel for suitability.

The senior specialist track is for those teachers who are steeped in their discipline and choose this route to become a "strong core of specialists with deep knowledge and skills in specific areas in education that will break new ground and keep Singapore at the leading edge" (Teo, 2001, as cited in Lee & Tan, 2010, p. 3), areas such as curriculum, planning, educational programs, and educational technology. Their leadership role takes them beyond the school to the ministry's headquarters where they may be engaged with curriculum development and evaluation. The ministry sponsors the postgraduate studies of these specialists in areas like curriculum, applied psychology in education, and educational research, and evaluation and measurement.

The leadership track is for teachers who have the aptitude and capabilities to take on school administration roles and is a pathway that could take them beyond leadership in schools to leadership at the ministry level. When teachers pursue the leadership track, they progress from teacher to subject head, head of department, vice principal, and then principal. As leadership is seen as a key enabler for effective schools, much attention and resources are given to identify and groom school leaders. All principals and department heads are fully trained at government expense before they take on their posts. Leaders are identified, cultivated, and recruited from a pool of teachers who demonstrate potential to take on school leadership roles. Each year, teachers are appraised on their leadership skills as well as their teaching skills in a multifaceted, competency-based process, and the ministry keeps tabs on up-and-coming potential leaders, reviewing appraisals, and checking in regularly with principals about which teacher is ready for additional challenges and learning opportunities. When potential principals are identified, they are given opportunities to take on new responsibilities and to engage in various kinds of training to further develop their leadership and management competencies. There is a comprehensive suite of leadership development programs planned centrally by the ministry, and customized suitably for new and experienced department heads, vice principals, and principals. At appropriate junctures in their careers, leaders are also assigned mentors to guide and coach them in their leadership roles. Officers undergo a rigorous selection process, after which they are appointed to school leadership positions when deemed suitable by the panel of appraisers.

The deployment of principals takes into consideration each school's unique leadership needs and the principals' experience and fit for each school. Principals are typically rotated after four to eight years in a school. This gives them sufficient time to initiate, implement, and consolidate new programs for the school. Principal rotation thus supports the ministry's goal of "Every School a Good School," enabling principals to contribute their knowledge and experience in different school contexts and bring fresh perspectives and best practices to their schools. It also provides principals with the opportunity to take on different challenges as part of their professional development.

The ministry-based pathway should not be seen as a separate leadership pathway for teachers, but rather a part of the continuum of leadership routes available to teachers. Thus, teachers who find themselves on this pathway typically have come from one of the other two pathways described earlier. One clear example of this is the establishment of AST in 2010. AST supports

> the professional learning and development of teachers by drawing out pedagogical leadership from the fraternity, infusing expertise into the system, imbuing a sense of pride, identity, and ownership among teachers, strengthening content mastery, building instructional capacity, raising the standards of practice, driving pedagogical innovations and change, advancing continuous learning.
>
> (Tan & Wong, 2012, pp. 452–453)

The idea of pedagogical leadership brings the skill and knowledge of senior, lead, and master teachers to bear on reform and improvement across the Singapore school system. However, the academies and language centers are not just places where senior teachers lead and junior teachers follow, but rather the mantra, "for teachers, by teachers. . . epitomizes the [MOE's] commitment and dedication to teacher professionalism, professional identity, and to the growth and lifelong learning of teachers" (Tan & Wong, 2012, p. 452). Consequently, the academies and language centers support teachers in learning communities and sponsor numerous teacher networks developed around mutual interest, needs, or disciplines. As noted earlier, these teacher networks are typically categorized as NLCs organized (1) by subjects (e.g., subject chapters), (2) by roles (e.g., school staff developer NLC, strategies for effective and engaged development [SEED] teachers NLC), and (3) by interest (e.g., normal course NLC [students in the normal course follow either the normal {academic} or normal {technical} curriculum, lesson study in chemistry NLC]).

The ministry is invested in expanding leadership opportunities for teachers at the system-level and so have announced:

> More leadership and specialist positions will also be created in MOE HQ as part of MOE's efforts to expand organisational capabilities and deepen expertise in the education domain to better support our teachers in our schools. All these will expand the advancement pathways for teachers and enrich their career experience.
>
> (MOE, 2011)

These leadership positions at MOE HQ ensure that teachers have a voice in policy and program development, as well as practice, and are engaged in reform efforts across schools, not just their own setting. Teachers can apply for these positions and try them on for size in two- or four-year stints. The positions are not only available at the ministry but also at NIE, thus affording teachers the opportunity to affect the next generation of teachers as university instructors in preservice teacher preparation. After testing these particular leadership waters, if teachers decide against these pathways, they are welcome back into the classroom, having expanded their perspectives and knowledge through engagement in diverse settings and activities.

We have introduced how Singapore not only ensures a smooth induction for all its teachers, but also provides all types of structures and opportunities for career-long professional learning. Now we move on to explicate how Singapore initiates educational improvement at the system and institutional levels, focusing on its review and reform in teacher education and the role of research in providing evidence for educational change.

THEME 5: LEARNING SYSTEM AND LEARNING PROFESSION

Review and Enhancement of Initial Teacher Preparation Programs: Maintaining Quality

The systemic approach to the preparation of teachers is undergirded by evaluation procedures and processes intentionally designed to be both educative and developmental. Characteristically, NIE engages in ongoing self-study: continuous learning, reflection, and evaluation for the purpose of renewal of its teacher preparation curriculum. A major overhaul took place in 2001 with the specific aim of integrating content and pedagogical preparation. This was reflected structurally with the joint location of content and pedagogy specialists in the same NIE academic groups or departments, which helped strengthen these ties. Since 2001, the institution has substantially revised the preservice preparation curriculum twice. In 2004, the institution undertook a comprehensive review of its ITP programs "to re-focus teacher preparation as teacher 'education' rather than teacher 'training'. . .[and] articulat[e] the desired attributes of a beginning teacher" (Chong & Cheah, 2009, p. 2).

In order to ensure abundance, diversity, and depth in terms of expertise, data, models, practices, and ideas, NIE's self-study method was typically multilayered, employing an "Expert consensus-building approach. . .[a] Research-based approach. . .[a] Professional Consensus approach" (Chong & Cheah, 2009, p. 2). The institution consulted with local and international experts on teacher education, as well as with key stakeholders such as principals and teachers. From this extensive examination came the Values, Skills, and Knowledge (VSK) framework for ITP, followed in 2008 by another effort to "reflect, review, refresh, and recharge. . .[so as]. . . to enhance the structure and substance of our TE (teacher education) model including program design and delivery, curriculum and pedagogical innovations, and preserve, build, and continually develop a culture of great respect for learning" (NIE, 2009, pp. 9–10).

NIE's 2008 review was guided by MOE's articulation of 21st-century competencies (21CC) presented earlier. Key characteristics of outstanding teacher education programs were also studied in the review process:

> seamless integration of courses that constructs a consistent learning environment throughout the program; comprehensible standards of practices and performance; a core curriculum with emphasis on student learning, assessment, and content pedagogy; use of problem-based teaching methods; active assessment using case studies and portfolios, drawing on the best practices of skilled veteran teachers in clinical experiences; and extending the amount of clinical exposure in the program.
>
> (Darling-Hammond, as cited in NIE, 2009, p. 7)

NIE took on board these research findings to enhance its TE model in order to prepare teachers who are able to meet the challenges of preparing their students for the realities of the 21st-century global workplace and society, resulting in the articulation of TE^{21}, Teacher Education for the 21st Century.

Researching into Practice for Practice

Learning as a profession does not stop at just the level of developing teachers as professionals and allowing their careers to grow along differentiated career tracks. More importantly, the system is keen to research into practice in order to find out what works, what does not, and what needs tweaking and refinement.

A systematic research program in the area of teacher learning, spanning from ITP through to the formative years as the BTs become professional teachers, is also critical. To this end, a number of competitively funded research projects on evidence-based initial teacher education and evaluation of the impact of key TE^{21} initiatives have provided the basis for future directions. Apart from these studies, the Office of Strategic Planning and Academic Quality (SPAQ) based at NIE was established in March 2014 after a reorganization, to incorporate the two key functions of strategic planning and academic quality management into a single office. SPAQ has expanded its role to include strategic planning to tap the synergies and linkages between strategic planning and evidence-informed academic quality enhancement efforts. For example, SPAQ administers various surveys, including the Stakeholder Survey, the Program Evaluation Survey, and the Graduate Preparedness Survey, to assess the quality of teaching and learning at strategic points of the teacher development process, and to track the impact of the implementation efforts in NIE's teacher preparation programs. Apart from ensuring academic quality, SPAQ also conducts environmental scans in order to be able to design the institute's overall strategic goals and directions. SPAQ takes the lead in formulating NIE's long-term strategic plans; its role is presented in Figure 13.

At the national level, the curriculum policy office of MOE develops and reviews policies to ensure that schools adopt sound, balanced, purposeful, and effective curriculum, pedagogy, and assessment practices, which

Figure 13. Strategic Planning and Academic Quality Functions at NIE.

Source: NIE, n.d.d.

are aligned with national directions and aspirations. It also engages in research work to ensure that curriculum, pedagogy, and assessment policies are informed by sound educational thinking as well as prevailing trends and developments in both industry and the wider society which hold implications for education. It facilitates sound, balanced, purposeful, and effective curriculum; and pedagogy and assessment practices in schools through partnerships with relevant divisions, branches, and organizations NIE and the SEAB (MOE, n.d.c.).

DISCUSSION

This case study has been organized according to five major themes, and this section will recapitulate the key learnings from each of the themes covered.

A Clear Vision and Belief in the Centrality of Education

Just 50 years ago, when Singapore first attained independence, literacy rates were low. The newly formed government under the visionary leadership of Singapore's first prime minister, the late Mr. Lee Kuan Yew, saw the importance of education as being integrally tied to the nation building, and in the early post-independent years to be crucially tied to the nation's survival. People were the only natural asset that the country had, and to help its citizens to realize their full potential, education was seen to be the key. Today, 50 years later, Singapore's education system is one that stands tall among those of other developed nations. The belief in the centrality of education in nation building still holds, and teachers are seen as being crucial lynchpins to providing the best possible education for each child in school. MOE's various taglines reflect the role of teachers in nation building, namely, "teachers mold the future of our nation" and "teachers—shaping the future of the nation, one student at a time." Though the educational initiatives have changed according to changing national agendas, the centrality of education in nation building has always been the focus. With education tied so closely with national survival and now national success, it is no wonder that the system is always striving to improve and to scale new peaks of excellence.

A Systemic Approach to Innovation, Reform, and Change

There is systemic coherence and clear alignment of goals within the education system. The system is built on a common national vision as mentioned in the preceding paragraph with clearly identified educational goals and outcomes. This is coherently managed such that there is alignment among the different stakeholders that make up the system, which can be encapsulated by the Policies-Practice-Preparation (PPP) Model. There is a tight and close tripartite partnership among MOE, NIE, and the schools. This systemic coherence also ensures that there is fidelity in the implementation of educational policies and initiatives. There are also a range of policies that work in harmony to support the development of teachers and school leaders, including recruitment, teacher preparation, induction, professional development, appraisal, retention, and well-being.

Building and Sustaining a High-Quality Teaching Workforce

There is an unequivocal belief and focus that teachers form the bulwark of a high-quality education system. As such, the recruitment, preparation, and professional development of teachers are taken very seriously. At the systemic level, teaching is regarded as an attractive and highly respected profession. Teachers are selected from the top one-third of each cohort entering elementary school, and the actual percentage is even lower considering the numbers that make it through the selection interview. Teachers are well paid with salaries pegged to those of beginning accountants and engineers, while those with prior working experience are compensated accordingly. The well-being of teachers is also taken care of by the ministry to ensure that they stay long within the profession. With the deep respect that society has for teachers, it is not surprising that altruistic reasons for joining teaching still prevail, and this augurs well for the future growth of the profession as teachers have a strong sense of pride in their professional identity as teachers.

There is also evidence of strong and rigorous preservice teacher preparation that continues through to the teachers' professional learning while in-service. All teachers are prepared by NIE that has a values-anchored university-based program accompanied by a strong school-based practicum designed to prepare teachers in the values, skills, and knowledge necessary for facing 21st-century classrooms and learners. There is heavy investment in teachers' professional development in terms of time and funding. The structured mentoring program (SMP) helps to further hone the necessary knowledge and competencies for the beginning teacher, as they journey to become professional teachers. Mentoring is taken very seriously and offered at various levels across the system: the school, cluster, and the ministry levels. Mentorship preparation is also not left to chance, and mentors are prepared to assume their roles through professional development workshops and seminars. Again, there is clear systemic alignment between MOE, NIE, AST, and the other academies and language centers to work synergistically to meet teachers' educational and professional needs, to support teachers' advancement, and to respond to national educational imperatives and goals.

Teachers are viewed as autonomous and thinking professionals, and they engage in various forms of research and professional activities to examine and improve their practices. These are all centered on the holistic development of students. Teachers are also expected to meet high standards of practice and engage in continuous professional learning and development both individually and through various collaborative professional learning communities.

Appraisal that Is Educative and Developmental

The annual appraisal system brings recognition and performance-based compensation to reward high-performing teachers. At the same time, non-performing teachers can be asked to leave the profession, and this ensures that the continuous quality of the profession is maintained. The appraisal system is educative and developmental as teachers are encouraged to expand their teaching repertoire, select their career tracks, and take those developmental actions that lead to greater competence and higher advancement levels on the career ladder. Even those teachers who perform poorly are given support and opportunities to improve their practice before final decisions are made that help them find alternate vocational options. Most importantly, teachers are evaluated holistically rather than solely on gains in students' test scores.

A Learning System and a Learning Profession

Varied and vast local and international PD opportunities are open to teachers while in-service. Additionally, to allow teachers to fully realize their aspirations, there are multiple pathways for career development such as the teaching, leadership, and specialist tracks. Each of these are well remunerated and designed to be maximally comparable to each other.

The architecture and design of the Singapore education system foster a culture of continuous learning and a system that never stands still. The TSLN initiative encapsulates this vision. The system constantly conducts environmental scans to envisage future needs and has the capability to learn and enhance its programs. A case in point is NIE, where there is a culture of upholding academic quality and which guides the constant review and enhancement of all its programs. Most of all, the system is always learning from the good practices of other international systems in order to constantly stay ahead of the curve and to provide the best education possible for its citizens.

Conclusion: Future Challenges and Directions

With an education system that seems to depict an educational utopia, one might ask, "What are the challenges that lie ahead?"

In our interviews with the school personnel, one key issue raised by teachers is that of time. Teachers cited just too many demands and too little time to meet these demands. Reading the case study, it is clear that the demands on the average teacher in the system are multiple and extensive. At the same time, the pressure to perform at a level that allows them to obtain at least a decent annual appraisal is tremendous. The danger of not having sufficient time to accomplish all that is needed within the scope of a teacher's work is the possibility of deep teacher frustration. Hence, a very real challenge that the system has to address is how to avoid teacher burnout.

The second challenge is also related to time. The many educational initiatives mentioned in this case study seem to be taking place almost simultaneously. The danger of this simultaneity is that while policies are implemented with fidelity, there appears to be insufficient time for one policy to be implemented and its success evaluated before another policy appears on the scene with the urgency for immediate implementation. This can sometimes mean that insufficient time is assigned to assess policies that do not work so well on the ground and which require policy amendments or even reversals.

The third challenge has to do with the system allowing the space for innovation and creativity. Though the system emphasizes the holistic development of the individual rather than test scores per se, the reality is that many of the national examinations still serve as gateways to higher levels of study and that the grades one receives in crucial benchmarking examinations determine the type of future pathways open to one. The diverse pathways may also come with connotations of different levels of prestige associated with each of them, and there is still an unwritten desire for students to head for the pathway that is deemed most academically prestigious if their ability allows them to do so.

Next, the present emphasis is clearly on values education. However, the reality is that values are difficult to measure, and one wonders how the measurement of the success of a system based on values education might be assessed in the future. Another question that emerges is whether the measurement of the outcomes of values education is only possible in the longer term, in which case the recourse for systemic tweaks might come too late.

The high performance of Singaporean students has been shown to be linked to the extremely high performance of the top performers far outweighing the top performers in other systems. Put another way, there is still a tail of bottom-end performers that require attention, and how the system works on leveling up these bottom-end performers is a challenge. Consequently, how teachers are prepared to help these performers is also of key concern. At the system level, MOE has introduced a number of policies to support low performers including the Learning Support Program (LSP), Learning Support for Mathematics (LSM), and stronger support for English Language literacy and numeracy in primary and secondary schools. Students with special education needs in mainstream schools also receive additional help from teacher aides and specialists in remediation programs (e.g., dyslexia remediation). (For details of these leveling-up strategies for low performers and the effectiveness of some of them, refer to "Learning Support for Pupils," 2013; MOE, 2015; "School-based Dyslexia," 2014; Vaish, 2010.)

In the final analysis, the evolution of the Singapore education system that has allowed the nation to move from third world to first is astounding. However, change was not the result of a miracle, but has been the consequence of long-term reform, trials with some errors, and a vision that has focused on the long term. Still, what remains pressing is the concern about how to continually sustain this educational success for the next 50 years or more and to ensure that Singapore's education system allows the nation to stay globally relevant and competitive in the 21st century.

NOTES

1. The Desired Outcomes of Education (DOE) were first formulated in 1997, and the current revision was published online on 1 Dec 2009 at https://www.moe.gov.sg/education/education-system/desired-outcomes-of-education.
2. In Singapore, cocurricular activities for students are school based and managed by the teachers.
3. The Portraits of Practice/Professional Perspectives integrated into this case study are drawn from Raffles Girls, School (RGS) and Kranji Secondary School (KSS)—two sites that generously allowed our in-depth observations, interviews, and videotaping.
4. Only candidates who crossed over from the Dip Ed programs to the BA/BSc (Ed) programs will qualify for this salary if they do exceptionally well.
5. Unless otherwise stated, the information in this section has been culled from the NIE practicum website. For more information, please visit http://www.nie.edu.sg/practicum
6. Quantum of about USD $3,000 for individuals and between USD $3,000 and $10000 for teams.
7. TALIS 2013: http://www.oecd.org/edu/school/TALIS-2013-country-note-Singapore.pdf

Appendix

METHODOLOGY

THE INTERNATIONAL TEACHER POLICY STUDY employed a multimethod, multiple case study design in order to investigate the policies and practices that support teaching quality within education systems. Seven jurisdictions across five countries were selected for the study based upon their highly developed teaching policy systems, as well as indicators of student performance on international assessments such as PISA. In larger countries, both national and selected state or provincial policies were examined to develop an understanding of the policy system. In these cases, the state or province was treated as a case nested within the larger country case.

The same research design was followed in each jurisdiction, with adaptation to local circumstances. The research was conducted in several phases:

- First, we conducted extensive document analysis, including education policy documents and descriptions of curriculum, instruction, and professional development practices and programs in primary, secondary, and higher education institutions. Reviews of the academic literature within and about each jurisdiction were also completed.
- These were supplemented with analyses of international, national, and, where applicable, state data sources. Quantitative data were used to support document analysis prior to the interview phases, and later, to triangulate findings from interviews. Quantitative data sources consulted included PISA and TALIS, Singapore Department of Statistics, and data from government documents.
- Two interview phases were conducted in 2014, beginning with interviews with policy makers and education experts in each jurisdiction. This was followed by interviews with agency administrators, principals, teachers, teacher educators, and other education practitioners. In each case, interviews were audio- or video-recorded and transcribed for analysis.

- The interviews were supplemented with detailed observations of activities in schools and classrooms, along with other key meetings and professional learning events.

Each jurisdictional team consisted of one or more locally based researchers and one or more U.S.-based colleagues. This approach provided both an "insider" perspective and an external lens on the data in each. Key lessons and themes from the each jurisdictional case study have also been drawn together in a cross-case publication that serves as a companion to the individual studies.

In this case study of Singapore, we interviewed 10 respondents as follows: 4 school leaders, 1 research director, and 5 teachers.

Observations were conducted in Kranji Secondary School (KSS) and Raffles Girls' School (RGS). The schools were selected because they have different governing structures: government school versus independent school. At each school we interviewed the principal, a vice principal, and a teacher who was filmed for the "Day in the Life" video. Teachers from a range of experience levels and responsibilities were selected to provide contrasting perspectives. Other interview participants included master teachers at AST, the director of the pedagogical research lab at RGS, and the head of department for English at KSS.

Interview data were supplemented with qualitative data drawn primarily from observations of key meeting and learning events. Observations undertaken during school visits included video filming of various school activities, specifically lessons in progress, teacher professional learning activities, and cocurricular activities. Additional data sources also included teacher schedules.

REFERENCES

Academy of Singapore Teachers AST (2012). *Professional growth.* Retrieved from http://www.academyofsingaporeteachers.moe.gov.sg/professional-growth/professional-development-programmes/teacher-leaders-programme.

Academy of Singapore Teachers (AST). (n.d.b.). *Ethos of the teaching profession.* Retrieved from: http://www.academyofsingaporeteachers.moe.gov.sg/professional-excellence/ethos-of-the-teaching-profession.

Academy of Singapore Teachers (AST). (n.d.a.). *MOE Teacher Induction Framework.* Retrieved from: *http://www.academyofsingaporeteachers.moe.gov.sg/professional-growth/professional-development-programmes/moe-teacher-induction-framework.*

Academy of Singapore Teachers (AST). (n.d.c.). *Our mission and vision.* Retrieved from: http://www.academyofsingaporeteachers.moe.gov.sg/about-ast/our-mission-and-vision.

Bilton, T. (1977). *Introductory sociology.* London: Macmillan.

Boud, D., & Falchikov, N. (2007). *Rethinking assessment in higher education: Learning for longer term.* New York: Routledge.

Buchberger, F., Campos, B. P., Kallos, D., & Stephenson, J. (2000). *Green paper on teacher education in Europe: High quality teacher education for high quality education and training*: Umeå, Sweden: Thematic Network on Teacher Education in Europe.

Chetty, R., Friedman, J., & Rockoff, J. (2013). *Measuring the impact of teachers II: Teacher value-added and student outcomes in adulthood.* Cambridge, MA: National Bureau of Economic Research. Retrieved from: http://www.nber.org/papers/w19424.

Chong, S., & Cheah, H. M. (2009). A values, skills and knowledge framework for initial teacher preparation programmes. *Australian Journal of Teacher Education, 34*(3), 1–17. http://dx.doi.org/10.14221/ajte.2009v34n3.1.

Chong, S., & Tan, Y. K. (2006). *Supporting the beginning teacher in Singapore schools—The structured mentoring programme (SMP).* Paper presented at the APERA conference 2006, 28–30 November 2006, Hong Kong.

Retrieved from: http://edisdat.ied.edu.hk/pubarch/b15907314/full_paper/1226593489.pdf.

Chye, S., Zhou, M. M., Liu, W. C., Koh, C., & Chew, E. (2012). Eportfolios in initial teacher education in Singapore: methodological issues arising from initial attempts to make meaning of artifacts. In S. Ravet (Ed.), *Proceedings of ePIC 2012, the 10th International ePortfolio and Identity Conference, London, 9-10-11 July 2012* (pp. 54–57). Poitiers, France: ADPIOS.

Cochran-Smith, M., & Lytle, S. L. (1999). The teacher research movement: A decade later. *Educational Researcher*, *28*(7), 15–25.

Coughlan, S. (2015, May 13). Asia tops biggest global school rankings. *BBC News*. Retrieved from: http://www.bbc.com/news/business-32608772.

Danielson, C. (2007). *Enhancing professional practice: A framework for teaching*. Alexandria, VA: Association for Supervision and Curriculum Development (ASCD).

Darling-Hammond, L. (2000). Teacher quality and student achievement: A review of state policy evidence. *Education Policy Analysis Archives*, *8*(1). http://dx.doi.org/10.14507/epaa.v8n1.2000.

Darling-Hammond, L. (2006). *Powerful teacher education: Lessons from exemplary programs*. San Francisco, CA: Jossey-Bass.

Darling-Hammond, L. (2010). *The flat world and education: How America's commitment to equity will determine our future*. New York, NY: Teachers College Press.

Darling-Hammond, L., & Hammerness, K. (2005). The design of teacher education programmes. In L. Darling Hammond & J. Bransford (Eds.) *Preparing teachers for a changing world: What teachers should learn and be able to do* (pp. 390–441). San Francisco, CA: Jossey-Bass.

Davie, S. (October 5, 2014). Ministry scales down recruitment of teachers. *The Sunday Times*, p. 1.

Day, C., Kington, A., Stobart, G., & Sammons, P. (2006). The personal and professional selves of teachers: Stable and unstable identities. *British Educational Research Journal*, *32*(4), 601–616.

Department of Statistics, Singapore. (2010). *Census of population 2010: Statistical research 1 demographic characteristics, education, language and religion*. Singapore: Author. Retrieved from: http://www.singstat.gov.sg/publications/publications-and-papers/cop2010/census10_stat_release1.

Department of Statistics, Singapore (2016). *Population trends, 2016*. Singapore: Author. Retrieved from: http://www.singstat.gov.sg/docs/default-source/default-document-library/publications/publications_and_papers/population_and_population_structure/population2016.pdf.

Department of Statistics, Singapore. (n.d.). Latest data. Singapore: Author. Retrieved November 20, 2013 from: http://www.singstat.gov.sg/statistics/latest-data#14.

Gill, C. (2013). *Open access to legal materials in Singapore.* Research Collection Library. Retrieved from: http://ink.library.smu.edu.sg/library_research/25/

Goh, C. T. (1997). *Shaping our future: Thinking schools, learning nation.* Speech by Prime Minister Goh Chok Tong at the Opening of the 7th International Conference on Thinking, 2 June. Retrieved from: http://www.moe.gov.sg/media/speeches/1997/020697.htm.

Goh, C. B., & Gopinathan, S. (2008). The development of education in Singapore since 1965. In S. K. Lee, C. B. Goh, B. Fredriksen, & J. P. Tan (Eds.), *Toward a better future; Education and training for economic development in Singapore since 1965* (pp. 12–38). Washington, DC: The World Bank.

Goh, C. B., & Lee, S. K. (2008). Making teacher education responsive and relevant. In S. K. Lee, C. B. Goh, B. Fredriksen, & J. P. Tan (Eds.), *Toward a better future; Education and training for economic development in Singapore since 1965* (pp. 96–113). Washington, DC: The World Bank.

Goodlad, J., & McMannon, T. (2004). *The teaching career.* New York: Teachers College Press.

Goodwin, A. L. (2012). Quality teachers, Singapore style. In L. Darling-Hammond & A. Liberman (Eds.), *Teacher education around the world: Changing policies and practices* (pp. 22–43). London & New York: Routledge.

Gopinathan, S. (2007). Globalisation, the Singapore developmental state and education policy: A thesis revisited. *Globalisation, Societies and Education, 5*(1), 53–70.

Gu, Q., & Day, C. (2007). Teachers resilience: A necessary condition for effectiveness. *Teaching and Teacher Education, 23*(8), 1302–1316.

Hairon, S., Goh, J.W.P., & Teng, K.W.A. (2014). Professional learning communities in the teacher intership programme in Singapore. In C.D.J. Mora & K. Wood (Eds.), *Practical knowledge in teacher education: Approaches to teacher internship programmes* (pp. 195–209). London; New York: Routledge.

Hattie, J. (2003). *Teachers make a difference: What is the research evidence?* Retrieved from: https://www.det.nsw.edu.au/proflearn/docs/pdf/qt_hattie.pdf.

Heng, S. K. (2011, September 1). *Speech by Mr Heng Swee Keat, Minister for Education at the Opening Ceremony of the MOE Heritage Centre on 1 September, 2011 at 9.00 am.* Retrieved from: https://www.moe.gov.sg/news/speeches/speech-by-mr-heng-swee-keat–minister-for-education-at-the-opening-ceremony-of-the-moe-heritage-centre-on-1-september–2011-at-900-am.

Heng, S. K. (2012, September 12). *Keynote Address by Mr Heng Swee Keat, Minister for Education, at the Ministry of Education Work Plan Seminar, on Wednesday, 12 September 2012 at 9.20 am at Ngee Ann Polytechnic*

Convention Centre. Retrieved from: https://www.moe.gov.sg/news/speeches/keynote-address-by-mr-heng-swee-keat–minister-for-education–at-the-ministry-of-education-work-plan-seminar–on-wednesday–12-september-2012-at-920-am-at-ngee-ann-polytechnic-convention-centre.

Heng, S. K. (2014, August 26). *Opening address by Mr Heng Swee Keat, Minister for Education at the Singapore-Industry Scholarship (SGIS) Award Ceremony on 26 Aug 2014, 7.00pm, at Concorde Hotel*. Retrieved from: https://www.moe.gov.sg/news/speeches/opening-address-by-mr-heng-swee-keat--minister-for-education-at-the-singapore-industry-scholarship-sgis-award-ceremony-on-26-aug-2014–700pm--at-concorde-hotel.

Hogan, D., & Gopinathan, S. (2008). Knowledge management, sustainable innovation, and pre-service teacher education in Singapore. *Teachers & Teaching*, **14**(4), 369–384.

Hutchings, M. (2011). *What impact does the wider economic situation have on teachers' career decisions? A literature review*. London: Institute for Policy Studies in Education, London Metropolitan University.

Ingersoll, R. M. (2007). A comparative study of teacher preparation and qualifications in six nations. Consortium for Policy Research in Education. Retrieved from: http://www.cpre.org/images/stories/cpre_pdfs/sixnations_final.pdf.

International Alliance of Leading Education Institutes. (2008). *Transforming teacher education: Redefined professionals for 21st century schools*. Singapore: National Institute of Education.

International Reading Association. (2008). *Status of teacher education in the Asia-Pacific region*. New York: UNESCO.

Janas, M. (1996). Mentoring the mentor: A challenge for staff development. *Journal of Staff Development*, **17**(4), 2–5.

Learning support for pupils struggling with English literacy. (2013, January 28). Retrieved from: https://www.schoolbag.sg/story/learning-support-for-pupils-struggling-with-english-literacy.

Lee, H. L. (2004). *Our future of opportunity and promise. Singapore government press release*. Address by Prime Minister Lee Hsien Loong at the 2004 National Day Rally at the University Cultural Centre, National University of Singapore, 22 August. Retrieved from: http://www.nas.gov.sg/archivesonline/speeches/view-html?filename=2004083101.htm.

Lee, W. O. (1997). Social class, language and achievement. In G. A. Postiglione & W. O. Lee (Eds.), *Schooling in Hong Kong: Organisation, teaching and social context* (pp. 155–174). Hong Kong, SAR: Hong Kong University Press.

Lee, K.-E. C., & Tan, M. Y. (2010). *Rating teachers and rewarding teacher performance: The context of Singapore*. Paper presented at the Asia-Pacific Economic Cooperation (APEC) Conference on Replicating Exemplary

Practices in Mathematics Education, Koh Samui, Thailand, 7–12 March 2010.

Lee, S. K., & Low, E. L. (2014a). Balancing between theory and practice: Singapore's teacher education partnership model. In *Tuition* 16, Spring 2014. Retrieved from: https://set.et-foundation.co.uk/publications/in-tuition/intuition-16-spring-2014/opinion-balancing-between-theory-and-practice-singapore%E2%80%99s-teacher-education-partnership-model/.

Lee, S. K., & Low, E. L. (2014b). Conceptualising teacher preparation for educational innovation: Singapore's approach. In S. K. Lee, W. O. Lee & E. L. Low (Eds.), *Levelling up and sustaining educational achievement* (pp. 49–70). Singapore: Springer.

Liu, W. C., Tan, G.C.I., & Hairon, S. (2014). Developing teacher competency through practice in Singapore. In J.C.D. Mora & K. Wood (Eds.), *Practical knowledge in teacher education: Approaches to teacher internship programs* (pp. 109–126). Oxon & New York: Routledge.

Lortie, D. (1975). *School teacher: A sociological study*. Chicago, IL: University of Chicago Press.

Low, E. L. (2014). Singapore's English language policy and language teacher education: A foundation for its educational success. In S. K. Lee, W. O. Lee & E. L. Low (Eds.), *Educational Policy Innovations: Leveling up and sustaining educational achievement* (pp. 85–102). Singapore: Springer.

Low, E. L., Lim, S. K., Ch'ng, A., & Goh, K. C. (2011). Pre-service teachers' reasons for choosing teaching as a career in Singapore. *Asia Pacific Journal of Education*, *31*(2), 195–210.

Luke, A., Freebody, P., Shun, L., & Gopinathan, S. (2005). Towards research-based innovation and reform: Singapore schooling in transition. *Asia Pacific Journal of Education*, *25*(1), 5–28.

McKinsey and Company. (2007). *How the world's best-performing schools come out on top*. Retrieved from https://mckinseyonsociety.com/downloads/reports/Education/Worlds_School_Systems_Final.pdf.

McKinsey and Company. (2009). *Shaping the future: How good education systems can become great in the decade ahead: Report on the International Education Roundtable 7 July 2009, Singapore*. Retrieved from: http://www.eurekanet.ru/res_ru/0_hfile_1906_1.pdf.

Ministry of Education (MOE). (2007, December 28). *Putting people at the centre of the education enterprise: MOE unveils "Grow 2.0" package to further strengthen teacher development and recognition and philosophy for educational leadership*. Retrieved from http://www.moe.gov.sg/media/press/2007/pr20071228.htm.

Ministry of Education (MOE). (2008). *Contact: Teachers' digest*. Retrieved from: http://www.moe.gov.sg/teachers-digest/2008/pdf/contact_may08.pdf.

Ministry of Education (MOE). (2009). *Teaching as a career*. Retrieved from: http://www.moe.gov.sg/careers/teach.

Ministry of Education (MOE). (2011a, March 7). *New "Teach" framework to enhance the quality of the teaching force*. Retrieved from: http://www.moe.gov.sg/media/press/2011/03/new-teach-framework-to-enhance-quality-teaching-force.php.

Ministry of Education (MOE). (2011b, May 18). *Growing the teaching force towards reduction of class sizes and more customised teaching*. Retrieved from: https://www.facebook.com/notes/ministry-of-education-singapore/growing-the-teaching-force-towards-reduction-of-class-sizes-and-more-customised-/10150302451342004.

Ministry of Education (MOE). (2012a). *Report of the Committee on University Education Pathways Beyond 2015 (CUEP)*. Retrieved from: https://www.moe.gov.sg/media/press/files/2012/08/cuep-report-greater-diversity-more-opportunities.pdf.

Ministry of Education (MOE). (2012b). *Teacher growth model: Fact sheet*. Retrieved from: https://www.moe.gov.sg/media/press/files/2012/05/fact-sheet-teacher-growth-model.pdf.

Ministry of Education (MOE). (2013). *Education statistics digest 2013*. Retrieved from: http://www.moe.gov.sg/education/education-statistics-digest/files/esd-2013.pdf.

Ministry of Education (MOE). (2014). *Education statistics digest 2014*. Retrieved from: http://www.moe.gov.sg/education/education-statistics-digest/files/esd-2014.pdf.

Ministry of Education (MOE). (2015, March 6). *Infosheet on levelling up programmes in schools*. Retrieved from: http://sineducationlink.com.sg/infosheet-on-levelling-up-programmes-in-schools/.

Ministry of Education. (2016). *Education statistics digest 2016*. Retrieved from: https://www.moe.gov.sg/docs/default-source/document/publications/education-statistics-digest/esd-2016.pdf.

Ministry of Education (MOE). (n.d.a.). *About us*. Retrieved from: http://www.moe.gov.sg/about/.

Ministry of Education (MOE). (n.d.b.). *Career information*. Retrieved from: https://www.moe.gov.sg/careers/teach/career-information.

Ministry of Education (MOE). (n.d.c.). *Curriculum Policy Office*. Retrieved from: http://www.moe.gov.sg/about/org-structure/cpo/.

Ministry of Education (MOE). (n.d.d.). *Development programmes and post-graduate scholarship*. Retrieved from: https://www.moe.gov.sg/careers/teach/teaching-scholarships-awards/development-programmes-and-post-graduate-scholarship.

Ministry of Education (MOE). (n.d.e.). *Financial assistance*. Retrieved from: https://www.moe.gov.sg/education/financial-assistance.

Ministry of Education (MOE). (n.d.f.). *Integrated programmes*. Retrieved from: http://www.moe.gov.sg/education/secondary/other/integrated-programme/.

Ministry of Education (MOE). (n.d.g.). *The Singapore education landscape*. Retrieved from: https://www.moe.gov.sg/education/education-system.

Ministry of Education (MOE). (n.d.h.). *Special education*. Retrieved from: http://www.moe.gov.sg/education/special-education/.

Ministry of Education (MOE). (n.d.i.). *21st century competencies*. Retrieved from: http://www.moe.gov.sg/education/21cc/.

Ministry of Education (MOE) Heritage Centre. (n.d.). *About MOE Heritage Centre*. Retrieved on from: http://www.moeheritagecentre.sg/about.html.

Mullis, I.V.S., Martin, M.O., Foy, P., & Arora, A. (2012). *International results in mathematics*. Chestnut Hill, MA: TIMSS & PIRLS International Study Center, Boston College.

Mullis, I.V.S., Martin, M.O., Foy, P., & Drucker, K.T. (2012). *PIRLS 2011 international results in reading*. Chestnut Hill, MA: TIMSS & PIRLS International Study Center, Boston College.

National Center for Education Statistics. (2009). *U.S. performance across international assessments of student achievement*. Washington, DC: National Center for Education Statistics.

National Institute of Education (NIE). (2009). *TE21: A teacher education model for the 21st century*. Singapore: National Institute of Education.

National Institute of Education (NIE). (2012). *A teacher education model for the 21st century (TE21): NIE's journey from concept to realisation—An implementation report*. Singapore: National Institute of Education. Retrieved from: https://www.nie.edu.sg/docs/default-source/nie-files/booklet_web.pdf?sfvrsn=2.

National Institute of Education (NIE). (2014). *General information Jan—Dec 2014*. Retrieved from: http://www.nie.edu.sg/docs/default-source/nie-files/te_admission/general-information_jan-dec_2014.pdf?sfvrsn=2.

National Institute of Education (NIE). (n.d.a). *Leaders in Education Programme*. Retrieved from: http://www.nie.edu.sg/leadership-professional-development/leadership-programmes/leaders-in-education-programme.

National Institute of Education (NIE). (n.d.b). *MOE sponsored graduate teachers*. Retrieved from: http://www.nie.edu.sg/higher-degrees/admissions/moe-sponsored-graduate-teachers.

National Institute of Education (NIE). (n.d.c.). *NTU-NIE Teaching Scholarship Programme-Empowering to empower*. Singapore: National Institute of Education, Nanyang Technological University.

National Institute of Education (NIE). (n.d.d.). *Office of Strategic Planning and Academic Quality*. Retrieved from: http://www.nie.edu.sg/docs/default-source/default-document-library/spaq-functions-4.jpeg?sfvrsn=0.

National Institute of Education (NIE). (n.d.e.). *Office of Teacher Education*. Retrieved from: http://www.nie.edu.sg/our-people/programme-offices/office-of-teacher-education.

National Institute of Education (NIE). (n.d.f). *Senior Teachers Programme (STP)*. Retrieved from: http://www.nie.edu.sg/our-people/academic-groups/policy-and-leadership-studies/programmes/senior-teachers-programme-stp.

National Institute of Education (NIE). (n.d.g.). *Undergraduate programmes*. Retrieved from: http://www.nie.edu.sg/teacher-education/practicum/practicum-structure/undergraduate-programmes.

National Institute of Education (NIE). (2015). *Bachelor of Arts (Education) / Bachelor of Science (Education) 2015-2016*. Retrieved from: http://www.nie.edu.sg/docs/default-source/ote-documents/programme-booklets/babsc_programmes_ay2015-2016_as-at-02-december-2016_latest.pdf?sfvrsn=2.

Ng, E.H. (2008). *Speech by Dr Ng Eng Hen, Minister for Education, and Second Minister for Defence, at the 11th Appointment Ceremony for Principals on Tuesday, 30 December 2008*. Retrieved from: http://www.moe.gov.sg/media/speeches/2008/12/30/speech-by-dr-ng-eng-hen-at-the-16.php.

Ng, P. T. (2008). Educational reform in Singapore: From quantity to quality. *Educational Research for Policy & Practice*, *7*(1), 5–15.

OECD. (2010). *PISA 2009 results: Overcoming social background—Equity in learning opportunities and outcomes*. Paris: Author. Retrieved on August 05 2015 from: http://www.oecd.org/pisa/pisaproducts/48852584.pdf.

OECD. (2014a). *PISA 2012 results in focus: What 15-year-olds know and what they can do with what they know*. Retrieved from: http://www.oecd.org/pisa/keyfindings/pisa-2012-results-overview.pdf.

OECD. (2014b). *Singapore: Key findings from the Teaching and Learning International Survey (TALIS)*. Retrieved from: http://www.oecd.org/edu/school/TALIS-2013-country-note-Singapore.pdf.

OECD. (2016). PISA 2015 results in focus. Retrieved from: https://www.oecd.org/pisa/pisa-2015-results-in-focus.pdf.

Provasnik, S., Malley, L., Stephens, M., Landeros, K., Perkins, R., and Tang, J.H. (2016). Highlights From TIMSS and TIMSS Advanced 2015: Mathematics and Science Achievement of U.S. Students in Grades 4 and 8 and in Advanced Courses at the End of High School in an International Context (NCES 2017-002). U.S. Department of Education, National Center for

Education Statistics. Washington, DC. Retrieved [date] from http://nces.ed.gov/pubsearch.

Quacquarelli Symonds. (2015). *QS world university rankings by subject 2015—Education.* Retrieved from: http://www.topuniversities.com/university-rankings/university-subject-rankings/2015/education-training#sorting=rank+region=+country=+faculty=+stars=false+search=.

School-based Dyslexia Remediation Programme (SDR). (2014, March 10). Retrieved from: https://www.schoolbag.sg/story/school-based-dyslexia-remediation-(sdr)-programme.

Sclafani, S., & Lim, E. (2008). *Rethinking human capital in education: Singapore as a model for human development.* Washington, DC: ASPEN Institute.

Siau, M. E. (2013, September 17). MPs call for closer look at private tuition industry. *Today.* Retrieved from: http://www.todayonline.com/singapore/mps-call-closer-look-private-tuition-industry-0.

SingTeach. (2010, May/June). Reflection: Thinking about doing. Singapore: National Institute of Education. Retrieved from: http://singteach.nie.edu.sg/issue24-teachered/.

Spillane, J. P. (2005). Distributed leadership. *The Educational Forum, 69*(2), 143–150.

Tan, C. (2005). Driven by pragmatism: Issues and challenges in an ability-driven education. In J. Tan, & P. T. Ng (Eds.), *Shaping Singapore's future: Thinking schools, learning nation* (pp. 5–21). Singapore: Prentice-Hall/Pearson.

Tan, K. S., & Wong, I.Y.F. (2012). Developing quality teachers for the Singapore school system: The Impact of the National Institute of Education and the tripartite relationship with the Ministry of Education and Schools. In I. Žogla & L. Rutka (Eds.), *Teachers' life-cycle from initial teacher education to experienced professional.* Paper presented at the ATEE 36th/2011 Annual Conference, Riga, 440–458. Brussels, Belgium: Association for Teacher Education in Europe.

Tan, O. S., & Liu, W. C. (2014). Developing effective teachers for the 21st century: A Singapore perspective. In O. S. Tan & W. C. Liu (Eds.), *Teacher effectiveness: Capacity building in a complex learning era* (pp. 139–157). Singapore: Cengage Learning.

Tan, O. S., Liu, W. C., & Low, E. L. (2012). Educational reforms and teacher education innovations in Singapore. In O. S. Tan (Ed.), *Teacher education frontiers: International perspectives on policy and practice for building new teacher competencies* (pp. 71–91). Singapore: Cengage Learning Asia Pte. Ltd.

Tan, Y. C. (2015). Preparing teachers for practitioner inquiry. *SingTeach*, 52. Retrieved from: http://singteach.nie.edu.sg/issue52-contributions/.

Teo, C. H. (2000). *Speech by Radm (NS) Teo Chee Hean, Minister for Education and Second Minister for Defense at the 2nd Teaching Scholarship Presentation Ceremony on July 15, 2000*. Retrieved from: http://www.moe.gov.sg/speeches/2000/sp15072000a.htm.

Teo, C. H. (2001). *Speech by Radm (NS) Teo Chee Hean, Minister for Education and Second Minister for Defence at the NIE teachers investiture ceremony on Wednesday, 4 July 2001 at 9.30 AM at the Singapore indoor stadium*. Retrieved from: http://www.moe.gov.sg/media/speeches/2001/sp04072001.htm.

Teo, C. H. (2002). *Speech by Radm (ns) Teo Chee Hean, Minister for Education and Second Minister for Defence at the second reading of the Republic Polytechnic Bill in Parliament on 8 July 2002*. Retrieved from: http://www.moe.gov.sg/media/speeches/2002/sp24072002a.htm.

The Holmes Group. (1986). *Tomorrow's teachers: A report of the Holmes Group*. East Lansing, MI: Author.

Vaish, V. (2010). A study of Singapore's Learning Support Programme: Educating from the heart. *Research Brief, No. 12–004*. Singapore: National Institute of Education. Retrieved from: https://repository.nie.edu.sg/bitstream/10497/6172/1/NIE_research_brief_12-004.pdf.

World Bank. (2008). *2005 International comparison program: Tables of final results*. Washington, DC: World Bank. Retrieved from: http://www.finfacts.ie/biz10/globalworldincomepercapita.htm#.

Yang, C. (2016, April 25). Student care centres for all primary schools by end-2020. *The Straits Times*. Retrieved from: http://www.straitstimes.com/singapore/student-care-centres-for-all-primary-schools-by-end-2020.

Yip, J.S.K., Eng, S. P., & Yap, J.Y.C. (1997). 25 years of education reform. In J. Tan, S. Gopinathan, & W. K. Ho (Eds.), *Education in Singapore: A book of readings* (pp. 3–32). Singapore: Prentice-Hall.

Printed and bound by CPI Group (UK) Ltd, Croydon, CR0 4YY
13/04/2025
14656500-0003